Practical Magick

THE ESSENTIAL
MIND BODY AND SPIRIT BOOKS

Practical Magick

Guidance, tools, spells

Hazel Cahill

ROCKPOOL

A Rockpool book
PO Box 252
Summer Hill
NSW 2130
Australia

rockpoolpublishing.com
Follow us! rockpoolpublishing
Tag your images with #rockpoolpublishing

ISBN: 9781923208957

Published in 2026 by Rockpool Publishing

Design and typesetting by Sara Lindberg, Rockpool Publishing
Edited by Amelia Willis

Caution: always check with your medical practitioner before using any herb if you are pregnant, breastfeeding, or have a medical condition. When burning candles, particularly when wrapped in anything, always ensure they are safely secured in a fireproof container and never leave unattended.

Printed and bound in China
10 9 8 7 6 5 4 3 2 1

Contents

Introduction

As you turn these pages, I invite you to open your heart and mind to the wonders of the magickal world. Each chapter is crafted to provide you with the knowledge and confidence to explore, experiment and grow.

Remember, the path of magick is a deeply personal and ever-evolving journey. Trust your intuition, honour your experience and let the wisdom of the natural world guide you. May this book be a source of inspiration, empowerment and transformation as you embrace your own magickal path.

Welcome to a world of endless possibilities and profound connection. Welcome to your magickal journey.

This book was born from hundreds of conversations, deep questions and quiet moments of reflection. Over the years, I've had countless people walk through the door of my spiritual business with quiet questions about energy, protection, grief and guidance. Some were curious, some were searching, some were in pain and others were simply drawn to something they couldn't quite explain. The questions they asked, the fears they held, the dreams they nurtured – they all stayed with me.

This book is a response to them all.

Whether you are a complete novice or a seasoned seeker, this book is designed to meet you exactly where you are on your journey. It offers practical wisdom, grounded advice and the reassurance that you are not alone as you navigate your spiritual path. You will find deep wisdom and a wealth of knowledge contained within.

My journey to magick

My path into magick wasn't linear. It wasn't something I inherited through a family line of witches or learnt through formal tradition.

It began in the quiet ache that something was missing. I wasn't satisfied with the superficial answers the world gave me. I longed for a connection with myself, nature and the unseen forces that I could feel but not yet name.

As a young woman, I was drawn to the natural world and ancient stories. Trees seemed to whisper secrets. The moon felt like an old friend. I collected herbs before I fully understood their power.

Working with herbs has had the biggest impact on my growth. Herbs taught me to listen to nature again, to slow down, observe the seasons and work in harmony with the land. Each plant carries its own wisdom and spirit, and learning to tune into this has been a profound part of my journey.

Like many of us, I learnt to hide my intuition for fear it would be dismissed or misunderstood, but life has a way of bringing us back to what's true. It was during a season of deep change that I turned fully towards magick. Not the kind of magick that's all glitter and moonlight, but the gritty, honest, healing kind. I began to study the old ways – Paganism, Druidic tradition, folk witchcraft – and I started blending herbs, crafting ritual tools and reading runes. I rediscovered a language that spoke to my soul and connected with others who were seeking just like me.

What began as a personal practice slowly grew into a business, a community and eventually a calling. Through workshops, talks, rituals and mentorship, I've now helped hundreds of people find clarity, courage and connection on their own paths.

What is practical magick?

While the title of this book may hint at a wide journey through various spiritual traditions – and yes, we do touch on many

– at its heart, this book revolves around one central theme: practical magick.

So, what do I mean by that?

Practical magick shows up in ways that are small but powerful, and you don't need expensive tools or complicated spells. This could be brewing a calming herbal tea before bed, placing a protective charm at your front door or taking a moment every morning to set an intention for how you want to feel that day. It could be in the way you speak to yourself, the energy you bring to your home or the rituals you create to mark transitions, no matter how simple they are. The most powerful magick often comes from your own presence and intention.

Practical magick is real, lived and grounded. It's not about grand gestures or aesthetic perfection. It is not reserved for those with elaborate altars or decades of study. It's the magick of everyday life: whether that may be grounding before a hard conversation, lighting a candle for courage or carrying a crystal in your pocket to remind you of your strength.

Practical magick is about reclaiming your power in a world that often tells you to shrink. This book reminds us that we are not separate from nature, that the cycles of the moon live in our bodies and that our intuition is a form of ancient wisdom. This book isn't here to tell you what to believe. It's here to give you the tools, ideas and inspiration to create your own path based on what feels true for you. I have shared rituals, reflections and 'real talk' not as a guru but as a guide who's walked this road too.

How to get the most out of this book

This book is designed to be flexible. You don't need to read it cover to cover in one go. You might want to start with the chapter that calls to you the most. Maybe you are craving protection, seeking clarity or just wish to understand what 'magick' even means.

Follow your curiosity. That's part of the magick!

Tips to get you started

- **Journal.** You may want to keep a journal nearby as many chapters include questions or practices that are worth reflecting on. Writing things down can help you process insights and track your growth.
- **Experiment.** If a ritual or a tool feels intriguing, try it. If something doesn't resonate, leave it. This isn't a rule book, it's a toolkit.
- **Use what you have.** Don't worry if you don't have fancy candles, rare herbs or expensive crystals. Magick lives in your intention. A stone from your garden, a tea light, a heartfelt prayer – they hold just as much power.
- **Reread with fresh eyes.** As you grow, the same chapter may hit differently the second or third time you read it. Let this book evolve with you.
- **Trust yourself.** There's no right way to be spiritual. The best teacher you'll ever have is your own inner knowing.

A final word before we begin

If you've picked up this book you're already on the path. You don't need to be more spiritual or better at meditation or less of a mess to be here. This journey isn't about becoming perfect; it's about becoming real. It's about remembering who you were before the world told you who to be.

Inside these pages you'll find everything from grounding rituals and lunar guidance to herbal wisdom and emotional healing practices. You'll learn how to blend the sacred with the everyday, how to bring magick into your home and how to tune into your own deep wisdom.

Some of this may affirm what you already know, some of it may challenge you, all of it is offered with love and respect.

So breathe deep.

You're exactly where you need to be.

Let's begin.

CHAPTER 1

Where do I start?

Beginning a magickal practice can feel both exciting and overwhelming. Many people sense a pull towards magick long before they understand what it is they are being called to explore. Starting out does not require special tools, advanced knowledge or a particular title. It begins with curiosity, awareness and a willingness to observe your inner and outer worlds. Magick grows through practice, reflection and patience, not perfection.

Answering the call

Often described as '*the call*' this moment can arrive quietly or dramatically. Some people call it a *spiritual awakening*. It may come through a sense of restlessness or a longing to connect with nature, ancestral roots or personal power. For others, it appears during times of change, loss or transition. Answering the call does not mean committing to a full-time fixed path. It simply means allowing yourself to explore what resonates and to learn at your own pace.

Types of witches

There is no single way to do magick, and many witches move between paths over time. Some feel drawn to nature-based or earth-centred practices, working with the seasons, plants and the elements. Others focus on folk magick, ancestral traditions or household rituals. You may encounter terms such as 'hedge witch', 'kitchen witch', 'green witch' or 'eclectic witch'. These labels are descriptive rather than restrictive. They are tools for understanding, not boxes to remain within.

Language and meanings

Magickal language can feel unfamiliar at first, but most terms are simpler than they appear. Words like 'ritual', 'intention', 'banishing' or 'cleansing' describe practical actions rather than mystical states. Learning the language of magick is not about memorising definitions, but about understanding how they govern focus and intent. This book introduces terminology gradually, explaining each concept as it becomes relevant.

Finding your way

There is no requirement to follow a single tradition. Personal responsibility matters far more than labels. Your practice may evolve, change direction or pause entirely at times. All of this is valid. Magick is a relationship with yourself, the natural world and the unseen, and like any relationship, it deepens through honesty, curiosity and lived experience.

Magic vs magick

'Magic' and 'magick' are often used interchangeably, but both describe the same practice: working with intention, symbolism, awareness and action to create change. 'Magick' is sometimes used to distinguish spiritual or ritual practice from stage illusion, but there is no difference in meaning here. What matters is the practice itself, not how the word is spelled.

Magick in the natural world

The natural world is essential to magick. It is a wellspring, offering the tools, symbols and energies that shape our practice. Every stone, leaf, flame, and drop of water carries its own vibration, and when we work with them in ritual, we are partnering with the earth itself.

Plants and herbs provide some of the most familiar tools: lavender to calm, rosemary to protect, sage to cleanse and rose for love.

From ancient apothecaries to modern witches' kitchens, herbs remind us that magick often begins in the garden. Trees, too, are sacred allies, oak for strength, willow for intuition and birch for new beginnings

Crystals and stones hold the slow, steady power of the earth. Each one is a vessel of energy: citrine for abundance, amethyst for clarity and obsidian for protection.

And the elements themselves become our tools: flame as fire, water in a chalice, incense or breath for air, and a cauldron, salt or soil for earth.

Even the moon and sun lend their light to charge spells, reminding us that our practice is never separate from the cosmos. By using what the natural world provides, we honour its gifts and recognise magick as a living partnership with the earth.

CHAPTER 2

Meditation, grounding and breathwork

Envision roots unfurling from your soles,
sinking deep into the dark, rich earth,
drawing up strength, stability and peace.

With every moment you stand connected,
the chaos within settles, the mind clears
and the heart remembers its rhythm.

Behold, the magick of grounding. Not merely a touch of bare feet to soil, but a sacred embrace between body and earth, a silent pact of belonging and balance.

Grounding is more than a spiritual act – it soothes the nervous system, steadies the breath and reminds every cell in your body that you are safe.

In the realm of the divine, grounding is the anchor that holds you steady as your spirit soars, the cord that ties you to the heartbeat of creation.

So, root deep, dear seeker, and let the earth hold you.

Grounding

Grounding is the practice of bringing your mind, body and energy fully into the present moment. In everyday life, our thoughts often scatter – worrying about the future, replaying the past or getting swept up in overstimulation. Grounding helps draw that scattered energy back into your body so you feel calm, centred and steady. It's like pressing an invisible reset button for your nervous system and spirit.

One of the best ways to ground is through contact between bare skin and the earth. Nature offers a constant, stabilising energy – it hums beneath your feet, flows through the roots of trees and shifts gently with the cycles of the seasons. Walking barefoot on grass or sand, leaning against a tree or simply breathing in the fresh scent of rain while observing your surroundings all help restore your inner balance and tune into the earth's steady, natural rhythm.

You don't have to be deep in the wilderness to ground yourself. Tending to houseplants, holding a stone or mindfully drinking a cup of herbal tea can be just as effective. The key is to engage your senses – feel the texture, notice the scent, hear the sounds around you and breathe steadily.

Grounding is a reminder that you are part of nature, not separate from it. By returning to that connection, you strengthen your sense of belonging. With time, you will move through life with a greater sense of calm, clarity and resilience.

Grounding in magickal practice

In spiritual practice, grounding is especially important before and after rituals, spellwork, meditation or energy work. Magick involves working with energy – raising it, shaping it and directing it towards your intention. Grounding helps you focus and stabilise that energy so it flows exactly where you want it to go.

Without it, you may find your energy scattered, your focus weakened, your emotions swinging or your results inconsistent, and you may even feel drained or dizzy after spellwork.

In magickal practice, this connection is more than symbolic. Nature is the original source of all magickal ingredients –

herbs, stones, water, fire – and aligning with it strengthens your own energy. By grounding through nature, you harmonise your personal vibration with the greater web of life, making your workings more potent and your intuition clearer.

Earthing

Earthing is a form of grounding that involves direct contact with the natural world, such as walking barefoot on the earth or consciously feeling the ground beneath you. Some practitioners prefer to begin with grounding as a way of settling the body and mind before any ritual work, while others find earthing most useful at the end of a ritual, as a means of returning to themselves and integrating the experience.

Grounding traces its roots to both ancient wisdom and modern science. Many spiritual and healing traditions, from Indigenous practices around the world to Eastern philosophies, have long taught that the earth provides a stabilising, nourishing energy.

Modern earthing research explores how this connection might affect human health. The earth maintains a natural, subtle electrical charge. Our bodies, too, carry electrical energy: every heartbeat, nerve impulse and thought depends on it. When we touch the ground directly, electrons from the earth can flow into our bodies.

Some researchers believe this exchange may help neutralise excess free radicals (unstable molecules linked to inflammation and aging) and restore the body's electrical balance. Small clinical studies have also shown that grounding sessions may reduce inflammation. Research findings also suggest grounding may promote deep sleep and regulate circadian rhythms, lower cortisol, reduce anxiety and provide some chronic pain relief, as well as supporting heart health and improving mood, energy and vitality.

While more large-scale research is needed, the results so far are promising – and the practice itself is simple, free and safe. Whether you view it through the lens of science or spirituality, grounding is a reminder that we are bioelectrical beings designed to live in harmony with the earth beneath our feet.

Learning the importance of grounding the hard way

There was a time, not long ago, when my days felt like a constant tug-of-war. I'd be in the shop chatting with a customer, all the while mentally running through what to make for dinner, worrying about the kids' homework and trying to remember if I'd paid the electricity bill. Add to that the occasional awkward conversation with difficult people and my energy was a tangled mess.

When I started taking my magickal practice more seriously, I noticed something. On the days I didn't ground myself, even simple rituals felt scattered. My focus would slip, I'd forget steps, and afterwards I'd feel oddly drained, as if I'd given away more energy than I had to spare.

One afternoon, after a particularly hectic morning in the shop and a heated phone call about school issues, I stepped outside with a cup of tea. I kicked off my shoes, just to feel the cool grass under my feet. At first, I stood there still buzzing with thoughts. Then I remembered the grounding technique I'd read about: imagining roots growing from the soles of my feet deep into the earth.

I tried it, half-sceptical, half-desperate for a reset. Something shifted. My breathing slowed, my shoulders dropped and that churning ball of worry in my chest eased. The problems didn't vanish – the bills still needed paying, the kids still needed dinner – but my mind felt clear and my feet steady beneath me. I walked back inside feeling anchored and ready to tackle the rest of the day, without feeling like I was about to tip over.

Now, grounding is as much a part of my practice as lighting a candle or casting a circle. I use it before seeing customers, before difficult conversations and especially before magickal work. It keeps me present with my children so I'm not just physically there but truly listening. It helps me hold my space in the shop when I'm surrounded by other people's energies, and it ensures that when I pour my heart into a ritual, my energy is focused and strong, not leaking in every direction.

For me, grounding isn't just a spiritual technique. It's survival. It's how I stay rooted in the middle of chaos, connected to the earth beneath me and steady enough to meet whatever or whoever walks through my door.

EXERCISE: STEP-BY-STEP GROUNDING

Grounding is most effective when it becomes part of your daily rhythm, not just something you turn to in times of stress. This exercise is one I use regularly, whether before magickal work, after a busy day in the shop or when life as a parent and business owner feels overwhelming.

You will need:

A quiet spot where you won't be disturbed. Outdoors is ideal – a garden, park, beach or even leaning against a tree. Indoors, you can stand barefoot on the floor or place your hands on a natural object like a stone or potted plant.

Instructions:

1. **Set your intention.** Grounding works best when you consciously invite it in. Close your eyes and silently set the intention: '*I am returning my energy to balance. I am steady, safe and connected to the earth.*'
2. **Feel your body.** Bring your awareness to your feet. Notice their weight against the ground, the texture beneath them – cool grass, warm sand, solid wood, carpet or tile. Let your attention travel slowly up your body, noticing any tension in your legs, hips, shoulders or jaw. As you notice these areas, imagine them softening.
3. **Focus on the soles of your feet.** Visualise roots extending from the soles of your feet deep into the earth. See them growing through soil and stone, eventually finding their way into the rich, nourishing layers below. You are now connected with Mother Earth: stable, calm and strong. Drink in the peace.
4. **Release what you don't need.** With each exhale, picture any stress, worry or scattered energy flowing down through your roots into the earth. The earth can transform this energy, just as it turns fallen leaves into fertile soil.
5. **Draw in energy.** With each inhale, imagine drawing up fresh, vibrant energy through your roots. Feel it rising into your feet, flowing up your legs, filling your entire body with steady, supportive power. Let this earth energy settle into your centre – just below your navel – becoming your personal anchor.
6. **Return to the moment.** Gently wiggle your fingers and toes. Open your eyes and take in your surroundings. Notice the colours, textures and scents around you. Feel the solidity of the ground beneath you.

7. **Seal the practice**. Thank the earth for its support. You may wish to press your palms briefly to the ground or to your heart as a sign of gratitude. If you're about to begin magickal work, you are now ready – calm, centred and focused. If you're returning to everyday life, carry this steady, rooted energy with you.

Grounding in this way takes only a few minutes, yet the shift in clarity, stability and presence can be profound. It is a reminder that your roots are always there, waiting to hold you.

Walking barefoot on the earth is one of the easiest ways to ground yourself and get the full effect of the energy of the earth beneath you. Mud, sand and earth will all have the same energetic benefits on your skin. Write how you felt below after your grounding exercise.

The magick and power of breath

Every time we breathe, we breathe in a portion of the outside world.

The purer the air, the better it serves us.

With every inhale, we take in the world around us. The air we breathe carries more than just oxygen. It contains the scent of rain on soil, the salt of the sea, the perfume of flowers and even the faint trace of far-off hills and forests. Breath is our most intimate exchange with the outside world, a constant dance between body and environment.

From a purely physical perspective, breathing sustains life. Oxygen fuels every cell in our body, supporting the brain, muscles and vital organs. The purer the air we breathe, the better it serves us. Clean, fresh air provides oxygen without the toxins and irritants that strain our systems. Polluted air forces the body to work harder to filter out harmful particles, impacting health, energy levels and even mood. This is why being in a forest, by the sea or in a space with good airflow can feel instantly rejuvenating: you are literally feeding your body with higher-quality fuel.

Spiritually and energetically, breath is the bridge between the seen and unseen worlds. Many traditions see breath as a carrier of life force – also known as prana, qi (chi) or simply spirit – that nourishes not just the body but the soul. When we breathe deeply and consciously, we are not only oxygenating our cells, we are also drawing in this subtle energy, replenishing ourselves on multiple levels.

Breathing connects us directly to nature's rhythms. The air we inhale has moved through forests, over oceans and through the lungs of countless living beings before reaching us. This shared breath is a reminder of our interconnection: we are never truly separate from the natural world.

Each breath is an act of receiving and giving, taking in what the earth offers and returning something in exchange. By slowing and deepening the breath, we calm the nervous system, quiet mental chatter and open the door to deeper states of awareness. Breathwork can clear stagnant energy, release emotional tension and sharpen focus before rituals or spellwork.

Pause to inhale fully, visualising yourself drawing in pure, golden light. Exhale slowly, imagining you are releasing heaviness and negativity. This is a simple but potent form of energy cleansing. In magickal practice, the breath can be used to charge an object. A whispered spell carried on the breath becomes more than words – it is infused with life force and released into the world to take root.

Every breath is a reminder that we are participants in a continuous exchange with the earth. To breathe consciously is to honour that connection. Air nourishes the body with purity and aligns our spirit with the steady, life-giving rhythm that sustains all living things.

Belly breathing

Most of us go through our days taking shallow breaths without realising it, drawing air only into the upper chest. This kind of breathing keeps us in a mild state of stress, signalling to the body that we need to stay alert, which can increase tension, fatigue and anxiety.

Belly breathing, also known as diaphragmatic breathing, is a simple yet powerful way to shift out of that stressed state and into one of calm focus.

Instead of breathing from the chest, we breathe deeply into the lower lungs, allowing the belly to rise and fall. This engages the diaphragm – a large, dome-shaped muscle beneath the lungs – which improves oxygen exchange, slows the heart rate and activates the body's relaxation response.

For magickal or meditative work, belly breathing is especially important. It steadies the mind, grounds the energy and allows us to enter ritual space fully centred. It also creates a rhythm that can be used to raise, direct or release energy with intention.

Before beginning the following exercise, take a moment to notice your breath. Are you breathing shallowly from the chest or deeply from the belly? We'll now explore how to shift into a fuller, more nourishing breath.

EXERCISE: THE BELLY BREATH

To begin, take some time to ground. You can be seated or lying down. Take a deep inhale through the nose and into the belly. Feel your belly rise as it fills with positive breath. As you exhale out of your mouth, let your belly fall.

Let your eyes be drawn to the Celtic spiral. Meditate upon it.

What does it bring to your mind's eye? Write what you see around the spiral.

EXERCISE: INTERNALISE THE LEARNING

The following is a short grounding and visualisation exercise designed to help you shift from reading into direct experience.

1. Close your eyes.
2. Take a deep breath.
3. Count backwards from five.
4. Open your eyes.
5. Which quote draws you?

> *'I welcome blessings with a thankful heart.'*
> *'I am on the path to healing.'*
> *'I am supported by the universe.'*

These quotes are offered as a moment of reflection. Read them slowly and notice how your breath responds, whether it softens, deepens or briefly catches.

You don't need to analyse why, simply observe what you are drawn to. Intuition speaks quietly before it becomes conscious understanding.

CHAPTER 3

Manifesting balance

Behold the power of manifestation.

Living in the thought of what is forming, moving with ghostly ease, embracing the feeling of what we seek as though it already breathes.

I return to the power of the self, not borrowed, not deferred, but held. Anew, I step into the state of having and the world will adjust accordingly.

Not merely wishing on stars, manifestation is a quiet, unwavering conversation between your heart and the universe.

It begins with stillness: the moment you dare to name what you truly desire and believe it has already begun to take form. Thought becomes thread, and the thread weaves through the universe into reality. Each intention is a stitch in the grand tapestry of your life. It is the warmth in your chest when you imagine holding the thing you seek, the certainty in your bones that it is on its way.

This is not empty hope, but the art of aligning your energy so the world recognises you as the keeper of your dreams. So, speak softly to the unseen, trust the timing and watch as the path unfolds before you, lit by the light of your own belief.

To manifest your desires, fill the spell bottle below with your intentions.

How does manifestation work?

Manifestation is the act of bringing something into reality through the power of belief and thought. The practice is based on the 'Law of Attraction', which says that thought and belief attract the real thing: you are living in the reality you wish to create. You believe that you already have that which you wish to manifest, and your belief sends the thought out into the universe.

Affirmations

An affirmation is a seed of thought, planted with intention into the fertile soil of the mind. With each repetition, the seed takes root, shaping the way we see ourselves and the world around us. Affirmations are tools of transformation, gentle yet powerful, that guide us towards a brighter mindset and open the door to possibility.

The voice we use when speaking to ourselves matters. Self-talk can be a friend that lifts us or a shadow that weighs us down. Choosing affirmations is choosing to speak with kindness, to replace old patterns of doubt with words of encouragement. The shift is not always easy. The mind may slip back into negativity, and that is natural. Yet each time we return to an affirmation, we are choosing growth over fear.

Affirmations can be created for every part of life, including success, finances, career, health, love and relationships. They remind us that even the most optimistic souls encounter moments of darkness, but words can light the path again.

Mantras

Similar to affirmations, a mantra is a word or phrase that is repeated to enhance an intention. Mantras are particularly repeated in meditation practice.

Some examples of mantras are

- *'I am rooted. I am steady. I am safe.'*
- *'I am allowed to pause.'*
- *'I move slowly with intention.'*
- *'I am supported by the earth beneath me.'*

Creating your own

An affirmation is a short, positive statement, such as '*I am successful*', '*I love and appreciate myself*', or '*I achieve my goals*'. These might seem like small, empty phrases – yet spoken with belief, they carry the power to reshape everything.

The key to successful affirmations is to believe in what you are saying and to repeat them consistently – daily if need be. With time, daily affirmations will help you shift your mindset and create a more fulfilling and joyful life.

When creating affirmations, keep them simple, clear and written in the present tense. Use positive language and focus on what you wish to invite, not what you want to avoid. For example, instead of '*I don't want to struggle with money*', write '*Abundance flows to me with ease*'.

Affirmations work best when they feel believable yet expansive, stretching you towards growth without creating resistance.

Begin with phrases '*I am*' or '*I welcome*' to ground your words in the now. Choose short, clear words that uplift you. The clearer and kinder your language, the stronger the energy it carries. Let the words flow naturally.

You might write them in your journal or on small slips of coloured paper, and place them where you will see them often – on mirrors, the backs of doors, inside cupboards or tucked beside your bed. Each time your eyes rest upon them, they will serve as a gentle reminder of your intention. These small notes will become daily sparks of encouragement, steadily reshaping your inner dialogue and anchoring your belief in the life you are creating.

Write your own affirmations in the box below.

Vision boards

A vision board is a map of the quiet whispers of your heart, a tapestry woven from dreams, longings and the secret songs of your soul.

With each image, word and symbol you place upon your vision board, you are planting seeds of intention. Each picture becomes a doorway to possibility, each word, a charm that calls your future closer.

Creating a vision board is the art of seeing with your spirit's eyes, gathering fragments of the life you desire and arranging them in a way that speaks back whenever doubt drifts near. A vision board does not merely decorate a wall: it breathes hope into the everyday, reminding you of where you are going and of the magick you already carry within.

On my vision board, I placed a house. Not bricks and mortar, but a dream house, walls woven from longing, a roof stitched with hope. I found images of gardens blooming wild and free, a front door painted a welcoming colour and windows spilling sunlight like blessings.

I added words that felt like spells: haven, sanctuary, home-coming. Each time I looked at my vision board, the dream rooted more deeply within me, as though the seeds of my future were planted in my soul.

Although I am not there yet, in quiet moments I can almost hear the creak of the floorboards and the rustle of leaves beyond the window. In stillness I hear the hush of belonging that waits for me …

A vision board makes the unseen tangible and gives breath to the not-yet. It teaches us to walk with faith beside our dreams and reminds us that the future is not so far away. What we call to with love will one day call us home.

EXERCISE: CREATE YOUR OWN VISION BOARD

Craft a canvas of an enchanting future, full of images and words, entwined with your intentions and desires.

Begin by drawing or writing in the boxes below what you would like to manifest. When you feel ready, create a physical or digital vision board of your own.

CHAPTER 4

The chakras

Breathe in earth, red and strong.

Breathe out fear, you belong.

Orange flows, waters move.

Golden fire, strength to prove.

Green heart opens, love is near.

Blue voice rises, truth is clear.

Indigo visions softly guide.

Violet crown, spirit wide.

Breath unites, chakras aligned.

The chakras are part of an ancient spiritual system that originated in India. First described in the early traditions of Hinduism, chakras were later explored in Buddhist practices and adapted by new age philosophers and spiritual thinkers.

The word chakra means 'wheel' in Sanskrit, referring to seven spinning centres of energy that are said to form a column of energy from the base of the spine to the crown of the head. These energy centres are seen as vital to spiritual, emotional and physical wellbeing.

Chakras are not simply symbols. They are a map of human consciousness. Each chakra corresponds to a particular aspect of life: survival and grounding, creativity and flow, personal power, love, expression, vision and spiritual connection. They are like gateways that link the material body to the subtle body, the layer of energy that surrounds and infuses us. Just as organs and systems make up the physical body, the chakras are centres of power and flow in the energetic body.

Together, the seven chakras create what might be called an 'internal circle' or a ladder of light within us. The lower chakras root us into the earth and into the physical world – our safety, sensuality and will. The middle chakras bridge earth and spirit, guiding love, compassion and truth. The higher chakras open into the realms of intuition and the divine. When energy flows freely through this internal circle, we experience balance, which manifests as a sense that we are aligned with ourselves, others and the wider universe.

Chakras help us understand that we are more than flesh and thought. We are beings of energy, constantly exchanging with the world around us. Our energy flows inward and outward, like tides, connecting the smallest aspects of our lives to the vast, unseen patterns of spirit. When we meditate on a chakra, we tune not only into ourselves, but the larger spiritual field that surrounds and sustains us.

Balance and imbalance

The chakras also offer us a language for understanding imbalance. For example, fear and anxiety may signal disharmony in the root chakra; difficulty speaking one's truth may point to a blocked throat chakra. By noticing these patterns, we can begin to restore balance through practices like breathwork, mantra, visualisation, sound and mindful living.

In this way, the chakras form both a practical and mystical system. Practically, they show us where we may need healing or attention. Spiritually, they remind us that our inner life is deeply linked to the greater currents of energy in the universe. The internal circle of energy within us is not separate from the cosmos; it is a reflection of it.

By honouring and working with our chakras, we strengthen this connection, remembering that we are both grounded in the earth and open to the infinite. The physical body depends on the balance of breath, blood and nourishment. In the same way, the energetic body depends on the harmony of its chakras.

When the chakras are open and aligned, energy flows freely from the base of the spine to the crown of the head, allowing us to feel grounded, centred and spiritually connected.

When the chakras fall out of balance, we may feel the effects in mind, body and spirit. A blocked or underactive chakra can leave us feeling stuck, fearful or disconnected, while an overactive chakra may create restlessness, overwhelm or imbalance in the opposite direction. These imbalances ripple through every part of life: relationships, creativity, confidence and spiritual clarity.

Balancing the chakras helps us to reclaim wholeness. Each chakra supports the others, and when one centre is brought into alignment, it strengthens the entire system. Together, the chakras create a flowing river of nourishing energy. A balanced system means we feel safe in the root, inspired in the sacral, empowered in the solar plexus, open in the heart, expressive in the throat, intuitive in the third eye and connected in the crown.

The chakras in spiritual practice

For those walking a magickal path, balance is not just desirable, it is essential. Magick requires energy, focus and clarity. When the chakras are balanced, we have a strong foundation to direct intention and power effectively. A grounded root chakra helps us anchor our spells in reality. A flowing sacral chakra fuels creativity in ritual. A confident solar plexus strengthens willpower and determination. An open heart chakra channels compassion and love into our work. A clear throat chakra allows us to speak words of power with conviction. A receptive third eye deepens intuition, guiding us in divination and subtle energy work. A balanced crown chakra connects us to higher wisdom, aligning our practice with the greater good.

Without balance, magickal practice may falter. Energy directed from a place of fear, resentment or disconnection can scatter or return in unintended ways. When the chakras are aligned, magick flows with greater ease, precision and integrity. The practitioner becomes a clear channel, harmonising inner energy with universal forces.

Balancing the chakras is, therefore, not just a practice of wellbeing, but also a sacred act of preparation. It ensures that when we step into ritual, meditation or spellwork, we do so from a place of harmony and strength. In this way, they are more than centres of energy: they become allies on the magickal path, reminding us that true power comes from balance and that the inner world must be aligned before we can shape the outer world.

The chakras and their associations

The crown chakra

- The gift of unity
- Located at the crown of the head
- Governs consciousness, thought and connection to the divine
- Resonates with the colour violet
- Crystal suggestions: amethyst, purple agate, purple aventurine
- Imbalance in the crown chakra manifests as disconnection from the divine, feeling abandoned by the universe, an inability to surrender or rest in uncertainty

The third-eye chakra

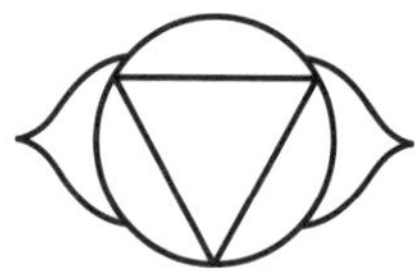

- The gift of seeing
- Located in the centre of the forehead
- Governs clairvoyance, intuition and imagination
- Resonates with the colour indigo
- Crystal suggestions: sodalite, lapis lazuli, azurite
- Imbalance manifests as failure to find a purpose in life, not seeing things clearly and memory difficulties

The throat chakra

- The gift of communication
- Located in the throat
- Governs communication and creativity
- Resonates with the colour blue
- Crystal suggestions: blue lace agate, aquamarine, blue howlite
- Imbalance manifests as difficulty speaking your truth and fear of public speaking

The heart chakra

- The source of love and key of healing
- Located to the left of the sternum
- Governs love
- Resonates with the colour green
- Crystal suggestions: green aventurine, rose quartz, rhodonite
- Imbalance manifests as loneliness, isolation, resentment, jealousy and being overly judgmental and negative

The solar plexus chakra

- The gift of identity: who we are
- Located in the solar plexus, just above the navel and below the rib cage

- Governs personal power, will power, self esteem
- Resonates with the colour yellow
- Crystal suggestions: yellow jasper, citrine, tiger's eye
- Imbalance manifests as mistrust and excessive concern about how others see us

The sacral chakra

- The centre of feelings, emotions and pleasures
- Located in the lower abdomen
- Governs vitality and sexuality
- Resonates with the colour orange
- Crystal suggestions: carnelian, orange calcite, garnet
- Imbalance manifests as negative thinking, fear of pleasure and fatigue

The root chakra

- The source of grounding and stability
- Located at the base of the spine
- Governs family, survival and roots
- Resonates with the colour red
- Crystal suggestions: black obsidian, black onyx, red jasper
- Imbalance manifests as fear, defensiveness, procrastination and unwillingness to commit

EXERCISE: EXPLORING YOUR CHAKRA SYSTEM

This exercise allows you to explore your chakra system through creativity, reflection and energy awareness.

You will need:

- A journal or sketchbook
- Coloured pens or pencils (red, orange, yellow, green, blue, indigo and violet or white)
- A quiet space where you will not be disturbed
- Optional: crystals connected to each chakra if you have them.

Instructions:

1. **Create your base drawing.** In your journal, draw an outline of a human figure, front-facing and centred on the page. It doesn't need to be artistic – a simple sketch will do. This figure represents you.
2. **Mark the chakras.** Using your coloured pens, mark the seven chakras along the body where they naturally align:

    Red at the base of the spine (root)
    Orange just below the navel (sacral)
    Yellow at the stomach (solar plexus)
    Green at the centre of the heart (heart)
    Blue at the throat (throat)
    Indigo at the forehead, between the brows (third eye)
    Violet or white at the crown of the head (crown)

3. **Tune into your energy.** Sit quietly with your drawing and breathe deeply. Place your chosen crystals nearby or hold one in your hand.
4. **Assess your energy.** Gaze at your illustration and, one by one, focus on each chakra. As you do, ask yourself: How does this part of my life feel? Is it flowing, blocked, overactive or undernourished?
5. **Reflect in your journal.** Beside your drawing, write down which chakras feel balanced and which may be out of harmony. For those that feel imbalanced, explore why you sense this. For example, if your heart chakra feels heavy, perhaps you've been struggling with forgiveness or feeling disconnected from others? If your solar plexus feels weak, you may be doubting your confidence or direction.
6. **Set an intention for balance**. For each chakra that feels out of balance, write a short affirmation or intention next to the chakra in the pen of the corresponding colour. For example:

    Root chakra: '*I am safe, grounded and secure.*'
    Heart chakra: '*I open myself to love and compassion.*'
    Throat chakra: '*I speak my truth with clarity and kindness.*'

7. **Closing the exercise**. When you are finished, place your crystals gently on the chakras in your drawing, as if charging them with energy. Sit for a few moments in quiet meditation, visualising each chakra glowing brightly and spinning with ease.

This practice brings awareness to your inner energy circle and helps you identify where balance is needed. It offers you a visual record of your journey to refer back to. Over time, repeat the exercise and notice how your chakras shift and realign as you grow.

CHAPTER 5

The nature of practical magick

When we light a candle, we call on fire.

When we draw a bath with herbs, we
invite water to cleanse and heal.

When we stand barefoot on the
earth, we ground our spirit.

When we speak words of power,
we ride the breath of air.

When we close our eyes and surrender
to stillness, we touch spirit.

To practice magick without nature is impossible. Nature provides all of the tools – the herbs, the stones, the cycles, the seasons, the elements – and more importantly, it provides the energy itself. Nature balances us. It reminds us that magick is not just about *desire* but relationship, not about taking but about co-creating.

To develop practical magick is to enter into dialogue with the world around you, to listen to the whispers of the wind, the songs of the trees, the wisdom of the moon and the steady heartbeat of the earth beneath your feet. In this practice we draw on a lineage of magickal knowledge from the Druids in pagan times to the Wiccans who reclaimed it. As we walk this path today, we are invited to remember it.

Magick is not something separate from the natural world. It *is* the natural world, seen with reverence, honoured with intention and woven into our daily lives.

Practical magick calls us back to this truth: every stone, every leaf, every breath of wind is sacred. And when we step into this relationship with respect and wonder, we find that the magick we seek has always been here, waiting in the earth, in the stars and in ourselves.

A legacy of earth-centred traditions

The importance of nature in magick is not a modern invention. For thousands of years, spiritual traditions across the world have found the sacred in the natural world. In Celtic lands, the Druids were known as keepers of nature's mysteries. They studied the movements of the stars and the moon, listened to the wisdom of the trees and worked with the elements in ritual and ceremony. For them, the forest was a temple and stone circles were gateways through which the earth's energy could be touched and guided.

Wiccan practice, which blossomed in the 20th century but drew deeply on older folk traditions, also places nature at its centre. Wiccans honour the moon's phases, celebrate the Wheel of the Year with its seasonal festivals and work with the five elements – earth, air, fire, water, and spirit – as essential building blocks of ritual. The Wiccan Rede, which calls us to '*harm none*', reflects the same respect for the natural order that the Druids once held.

Practical magick today draws from these roots. To practice it is to step into this lineage of earth-honouring spirituality, carrying forwards the understanding that the natural world is not only sacred but the very medium through which magick works.

The language of the natural world

One of the first steps on the path of practical magick is learning the language of nature. Plants, trees, animals and the moon all carry their own energy. By noticing them, you begin to see how they can become allies in your magickal work.

Every plant carries a spirit, a particular vibration. Calendula shines with joy and healing, rosemary protects and strengthens, oak stands firm as a guardian of endurance, and willow bends yet does not break, teaching us resilience. To the Druids, trees were sacred beings, each with their own wisdom. In working with plants, whether as herbs, incense or offerings, we are not just using ingredients: we are entering into a relationship with living forces.

Animals, too, embody qualities that guide us. The raven speaks of mystery and transformation, the deer of gentleness and grace, the wolf of loyalty and wild freedom. In Celtic lore, animals often acted as guides or messengers, leading heroes through the spirit world. Even today, paying attention to the animals that appear in our dreams or daily lives can offer insight into the energies moving through us.

The moon is perhaps the most constant companion of magickal practice. Her waxing, full, waning and dark phases provide a natural rhythm for spellwork – growth, manifestation, release and rest. The Druids tracked her cycles to mark time for rituals, while Wiccans honour the Esbats, or full moon celebrations, as moments of heightened magickal energy.

Finally, the elements of earth, air, fire, water and spirit underpin all practical magick. Earth grounds us in stability and growth. Air inspires thought and communication. Fire sparks passion and transformation. Water brings emotion, healing and intuition. Spirit is the unseen thread that binds all the elements together, connecting us to the divine. To work magick without understanding the elements is like trying to build a house without knowing how stone, wood and mortar fit together.

The forest embrace

There are places in this world where the noise softens, the rush of time slows and the body remembers what it is to belong. For me, that place has always been the forest. It begins the moment I step beneath the canopy, leaving behind the hard edges of pavements and the constant hum of traffic.

The air changes first. It cools instantly, as though the trees have drawn up all the harshness of the outside world and replaced it with a calm, clean breath. I feel the drop in temperature against my skin with relief, like plunging my hands into clear spring water.

The trees stand tall around me, their trunks forming ancient pillars that hold up a ceiling of leaves. As the wind moves, the branches sway and knit together in shifting patterns. The canopy is a living roof that shields me from the sun's glare and the weight of the world outside, like a protective blanket, draping me in safety.

No matter how unsettled my mind might feel when I arrive, the forest greets me with quiet steadiness and I can almost hear it whisper: '*You are safe here.*'

I breathe. Beneath my feet the earth is soft and forgiving. The ground is springy, padded with moss, pine needles and years of fallen leaves. With each step I sink ever so gently, walking on a natural carpet woven by time itself. There is comfort in that sensation, as if the land is cradling me and saying, '*You don't need to hold yourself so tightly anymore.*'

The deeper I walk, the more the outer world falls away. The sounds of engines and voices fade until all I hear is birdsong, the occasional rustle of a squirrel darting through the undergrowth and the steady rhythm of my own breath.

I feel the rise and fall of breath in my chest and the quiet pulse of my heartbeat in my ears. I am reminded that my body, often rushed, worried or pulled in too many directions, is still connected to the heartbeat of the earth. I am in the quiet embrace of the natural world.

What touches me most is the way the forest seems to know what I need. On days when my thoughts are crowded and tangled, the trees show me how to let go. They release their leaves without hesitation when the season calls for it, letting them drift down to nourish the soil.

Watching that cycle play out around me teaches me that it's safe to release what no longer serves me. I don't need to cling to every worry or carry every burden. I can drop them gently and trust they will decompose into wisdom to make space for new growth.

On other days, when I'm weighed down by self-doubt or heavy moods, I find strength in the roots that spread out of sight beneath me. They remind me that even if I can't see it, I too have roots – in my family, in my ancestors and in the earth itself. I am held by something greater than my current worries.

Sometimes I pause, close my eyes and simply lean against a tree. The bark is rough beneath my palms, grounding me, and I imagine its life force rising through its trunk like a slow river of light. I let myself feel part of that flow, letting it seep into me until my shoulders drop and my thoughts soften. In that moment, the forest and I are not separate – I am as much a part of it as the moss, the birdcalls or the breeze.

By the time I step back into the open air, the world hasn't changed, but I have. I carry with me the cool breath of leaves, the softness of the ground and the memory of that protective green canopy. The forest is a sanctuary, yes, but it is also a teacher, showing me how to live with resilience, how to let go and how to find steadiness even in the midst of life's storms.

In the end, connecting with nature isn't about escaping reality. It's about remembering that I am not separate from it, that my roots sink just as deeply, and that I too am woven into the great, protective blanket of the living earth.

EXERCISE: A WALK IN THE FOREST

This exercise is more than a simple walk. It is a gentle practice in connection, grounding and renewal. You can return to this whenever you need support from something greater than yourself. Nature is always waiting, ready to wrap you in its quiet, protective embrace.

1. **Begin with intention.** Before you step into the forest, pause at the threshold. It might be the car park, gate or the path that leads you under the trees. Place your hand over your heart and silently set an intention:
   '*I am here to reconnect, to feel the earth beneath me and to be held by nature*'.
2. **Cross the threshold.** As you enter, imagine you are walking through a doorway into a sacred space. Notice how the light shifts. The canopy of branches above becomes a vast, living

roof. They are a protective blanket of green that shields you from the harshness of the outside world. Allow yourself to feel safe here.

3. **Breathe the forest air.** Stop for a moment and take three slow breaths. Inhale deeply, letting the coolness of the forest air move into your lungs. Exhale slowly, releasing tension, worry or heaviness. As it passes through your nostrils, notice how the air feels different here: fresher, cooler and alive with the scent of leaves, bark and damp earth.
4. **Walk with awareness.** Begin to walk slowly along the path. With each step, notice how the ground feels beneath your feet. Perhaps it is soft, padded with moss and fallen leaves, or springy with pine needles. Imagine the earth rising up to meet you, supporting your body with every step. Allow your movements to slow until they match the quiet rhythm of the forest.
5. **Listen and observe.** Pause and let your senses expand. What sounds are alive around you? A bird's call, the whisper of branches, the distant rush of a stream? What can you see? Patterns of light through the trees, tiny plants growing in the shade, a flicker of movement in the undergrowth? Let your awareness wander gently, without needing to identify, label or analyse.
6. **Connect with a tree.** Softly notice a tree that calls to you. It might be tall and straight, gnarled and wise, or simply glowing in the light. Walk towards it and place your hand on its bark. Feel its texture, rough or smooth. Close your eyes and imagine its roots reaching deep into the soil, anchoring you too. Breathe with the tree, feeling its strength rise through your hand and into your body. As you touch the tree, know you are touched in return by its steady spirit.

7. **Offer gratitude.** When you are ready to leave, whisper a thank you to the trees, the air, the ground and the unseen spirits of the place. Gratitude completes the circle, sealing the connection between you and the living world.
8. **Carry the magick back.** As you step back into the everyday world, carry the forest within you. Remember the cool air, the soft ground and the sheltering canopy. When life feels heavy, you can close your eyes and return to that space in your mind, letting it remind you: '*You are held. You are supported. You belong.*'

The moon

The moon's divine energy is a deeply powerful presence in the magick of nature. As the moon waxes and wanes, she draws us into her gentle, luminous embrace. She moves the tides and stirs our spirits. Her rhythms echo within the hidden chambers of our hearts. Her shimmering is a reminder that mystery itself is power. When we open ourselves to her, we surrender to her boundless energy and allow her light to guide our path.

Throughout history, the moon has been honoured as feminine, cyclical, mysterious, transformative, intuitive, protective, fertile, guiding, reflective and eternal. Witches have long honoured the moon as a sacred guide, aligning spells with her cycles to amplify intention or worshipping her as goddesses such as Selene, Artemis, Hecate and Cerridwen.

The moon's phases provide natural rhythms for spellwork and each phase carries its own energy.

- **New moon:** planting seeds, beginnings, intention-setting
- **Waxing moon:** growth, attraction, building power
- **Full moon:** release, charging crystals, manifesting change, heightened energy
- **Waning moon:** integration, rest, clearing, winding down after the full moon

Magick aligns with the moon because she mirrors the cycles within us – birth, growth, fullness and release. By working in harmony with her phases, practitioners channel her power into their spells, drawing upon her energy to amplify intention and bring balance between the seen and unseen. We weave our magick into the eternal dance of light and shadow.

The full moon

The full moon reveals hidden or neglected parts of ourselves. This is the phase of starting anew, redefining the narrative and embarking on a fresh journey for the upcoming cycle.

Things to do on a full moon:

- Charge your tools or crystals by placing them where the full moon's light will shine upon them.
- Take a moon bath.
- Undertake divination rituals or read tarot cards.

- Make moon water by filling a vessel with filtered water, adding some salt or quartz crystals, and placing it overnight under the full moon.
- Write a gratitude list.

EXERCISE: A FULL MOON SPELL

You will need:

- A white candle to represent peace
- A green candle to represent abundance
- Herbs of your choice
- Pen and paper
- A lighter or matches and a heat-proof dish

Instructions:

1. Light your candles.
2. Sprinkle some herbs around the base of your candles.
3. Meditate on what it is you wish to let go of.
4. Write what you wish to release on the paper.
5. Fold the paper away from yourself to release the intention.
6. Burn the paper using the flame of your candle. Place your burning paper onto the heat-proof dish to burn out safely.
7. Sprinkle some of your herbs over the burning paper.

The new moon

The new moon symbolises a fresh start, making it an optimal time for planning, goal setting and manifesting desires. This is a great time to set an intention for the coming weeks.

Things to do on a new moon:

- Clean your altar and declutter your space.
- Set intentions for the cycle ahead.
- Delve into shadow work.
- Plant seeds in your garden.

EXERCISE: A NEW MOON SPELL

You will need:

- A green candle to represent abundance
- Herbs to enhance your intention
- Pen and paper
- A lighter or matches and a heat-proof dish

Instructions:

1. Light your candle.
2. Sprinkle some herbs around the base of your candle.
3. Write your intention for this new moon cycle on the paper.
4. Fold the paper towards you to bring in your intention.

5. Burn the paper using the flame of your candle, or you can carry your intention with you until the next full moon. If burning, place the paper onto a heat-proof dish to burn out safely.

Minor moon phases

The minor moon phases are the subtle moments in between the great turning points of the lunar cycle. They are like pauses between breaths – not as dramatic as the new or full moon, yet just as meaningful. These phases remind us that transformation is rarely instant; it unfolds in gentle increments, with space to pause, adjust and listen. Working with them encourages mindfulness, patience and trust in the process.

By honouring the quiet transitions, we attune ourselves to the natural ebb and flow of energy, discovering that magick often lies in the spaces between the extremes.

Here is what to focus on in each of the moon phases.

- **Waxing crescent:** refining, reassessing
- **Waxing half moon:** recommitment
- **Waxing gibbous:** resilience, trust
- **Waning gibbous:** gratitude, blessings
- **Waning half moon:** self-care
- **Waning crescent:** reflection

Spirit animals and nature spirits

Spirit animals are guides from the natural world who walk beside us in both seen and unseen ways. They are not pets, mascots or possessions, but allies: living symbols of qualities, lessons and energies that help us navigate our path.

Belief in animal guides runs deep across many cultures. In Celtic lore, stags, boars and ravens often appeared as messengers or protectors. In Native American traditions, totem animals embody wisdom and offer teachings to the tribe or individual. In shamanic practice worldwide, animals are seen as powerful companions who bridge the physical and spiritual realms.

A spirit animal is often recognised through repeated encounters. It might be a fox appearing in your dreams or an owl that crosses your path at significant moments. Does an animal stir something deep within your heart each time you meet it? This suggests the animal's energy is resonating with your own, calling your attention to lessons you may need.

Spirit animals connect us to the greater web of nature spirits. All of nature is alive: trees, rivers, mountains and winds carry energy and consciousness. Animals embody this aliveness in forms we can easily see and understand. Through them, the unseen becomes tangible.

When a wolf appears as a guide, it carries not only its own qualities of loyalty and instinct but also the voice of the wild forests it roams. When a hawk soars into our awareness, it brings with it the vastness of sky and sharpness of vision that only air spirits know.

Working with a spirit animal is a way of entering into dialogue with nature itself and deepening your connection to the spirits of the land. Meditating on your spirit animal allows you to tune into its wisdom. The fox teaches adaptability, the deer gentleness, the bear courage and the butterfly transformation. Each is a mirror of energies already within you, but awakened and sharpened through the relationship.

Spirit animals remind us that we are not separate from nature, but part of its great circle. They invite us to move with more awareness of our instincts, to live in harmony with our environment and to recognise the sacred in the creatures who share this earth with us. To honour your spirit animal – perhaps through art, offerings or simply gratitude – is to honour the spirit of nature itself.

Most importantly, spirit animals are not here to serve us or be dominated by us in any way. They come as companions and teachers, helping us walk our path with courage, intuition and respect. By listening to their messages, we learn to listen to the deeper song of the natural world, and in doing so, we align ourselves more closely with the great flow of spirit that moves through all life.

Spirit animals for protection and magick

Certain animals are seen as guardians and guides in magickal practice. They carry energies that shield, guide or awaken the inner sight of the practitioner. When these creatures appear in ritual, dreams or daily life, they remind you that you are watched over and supported. Here are just a few spirit animals that may appear to you. Chapters 11 and 12 explore further which spirit animals may assist you in different rituals and spells.

Black cat

Long associated with witches, mystery and the unseen, the black cat is a protector of magickal energy. It is said to keep harmful influences at bay, bring heightened intuition and psychic power, and ward off envy or ill intent. It is also said that stroking a black cat nine times brings good luck in love. The black cat is also sacred to many goddesses including Freyja and Bastet. Black cats are known to hold the spirit of the witch they belong to.

Owl

The owl is the seer of the night, offering wisdom and prophecy. The owl protects against deception and they can see through illusion and will guide you through darkness. The owl encourages clear-sightedness in divination and calls on you to trust your inner knowing.

Wolf

The guardian of the path, loyal and instinctual, the wolf protects the soul during transitions and dream journeys. The wolf defends against energetic intrusions and teaches you to trust your intuition and when to stand your ground.

Hawk/eagle

Birds of prey are messengers of vision and clarity. They protect against confusion or hidden threats and guide the practitioner to rise above current entanglements to see the bigger picture.

Stag/deer

The graceful, gentle stag (also sometimes appearing as a deer) is considered in Celtic lore to be a gatekeeper to other realms.

Stags protect sacred boundaries and lead seekers safely between worlds. They embody sovereignty, higher truths and dignity in magickal practice.

Snake

The snake is a symbol of transformation and hidden knowledge. Through its association with the ouroboros, snakes teach renewal and encourage shedding what no longer serves. They are known to guard the threshold of deeper mysteries.

Raven/crow

Messengers from other realms, omens and harbingers of change, ravens and crows are strongly tied to prophecy and represent death and rebirth. They warn of danger or unseen forces, are fiercely protective and will guide the witch through shadow work and transformation.

Bear

A guardian of strength, dreams and introspection, the bear protects through grounding and the fierce defence of boundaries. Bears support those working with vision quests or inner journeys, so call upon them in spellwork to stand at your side as guardians.

EXERCISE: FIND AND CONNECT WITH YOUR SPIRIT ANIMAL

Recognising your spirit animal often begins with noticing patterns. Perhaps a certain animal appears repeatedly in your dreams, visions or daily life. It may be a fox crossing your path at key moments or an owl whose call seems to follow you.

Sometimes the connection is subtler. You may have had a lifelong fascination with a creature or feel a sense of kinship or sudden surge of emotion when you feel the presence of a certain animal. These are whispers from the spirit world, nudging you to pay attention.

To connect more deeply to your guide, follow this meditation practice. You may also wish to use dreams as a gateway. Set the intention before you sleep to meet your spirit animal, then record the results when you wake.

You will need:

- A quiet space where you won't be disturbed
- Optional: candles, herbs, crystals or other ritual tools

Instructions:

1. Begin with meditation. Sit quietly and breathe deeply. Imagine yourself walking into a natural landscape, maybe a forest or a beach.
2. When you're ready, ask for your guide to reveal itself. Be patient – the first image you see is often the truest.
3. Once you recognise your guide, honour it. Learn about its habits in the natural world, reflect on the lessons it carries and consider how its qualities mirror your own life.
4. Offer gratitude to your guide. This could be through art, journalling or a simple acknowledgment. In doing so, you invite a relationship of respect, allowing your spirit animal to become an ally on your path.

CHAPTER 6

The five elements

Before all words, there were the elements:

the breath that moves,

the flame that warms,

the water that remembers,

and the earth that holds and endures.

To traverse the mystic realms of witchcraft, Wiccan and Pagan practices is to connect with the guiding hand of the universe's divine energy. At the core of this enchantment lie five elements, ancient and ever-present: earth, air, fire, water and spirit.

In the Wiccan tradition, each element is a thread in the tapestry of the universe, woven with a unique colour, herb, deity and astrological sign. As we honour each element, we honour the sacred balance of existence itself.

The elements are central to casting a circle – a sacred space between worlds – in Wiccan and other Pagan practices. Many shaman practitioners also call the quarters, inviting earth in the north, air in the east, fire in the south and water in the west, with spirit above and within. Each element guards and balances the circle, creating a protective boundary and weaving harmony into the ritual.

Earth

Earth is the element of stability, grounding and manifestation. It is the soil beneath our feet, the bones of our body and the endurance of stone and mountain. In magick, earth governs prosperity, abundance, growth and protection. Its correspondences are green and brown, salt, patchouli, oak and the north. When you call on earth in ritual, you call strength, patience and the power to bring dreams into tangible form.

Air

Air is the element of thought, communication and inspiration. It is the breath that animates us, the whisper of wind and the clarity of the sky. Air governs knowledge, divination, creativity and new beginnings. Its correspondences are yellow, incense, lavender, feathers and the east. When you invoke air, you invite in fresh ideas, clarity of mind and the power of your words.

Fire

Fire is the element of passion, transformation and will. It is the flame of the candle, the spark of creation and the blaze that burns away what no longer serves. In magick, fire governs courage, sexuality, energy and purification. Its correspondences are red and orange, candles, cinnamon, dragons and the south. Calling on fire in ritual ignites determination, fuels magick with power and channels raw energy into change.

Water

Water is the element of emotion, intuition and healing. Flowing in rivers, tides and tears, it reminds us of life's ebb and flow. Water governs love, dreams, psychic work and purification. Its correspondences are blue, seashells, rose, myrrh and the west. In ritual, water is invoked to cleanse, bless and to open the heart to compassion and empathy.

Spirit

Spirit is the binding force, the element beyond elements and the spark of divinity that threads through all things. It has no fixed colour or direction, though often it is visualised as white, purple or violet, or a shining golden light. Spirit represents connection to the divine, the higher self and the unseen web that unites the other four. It reminds us that we are part of a greater whole. Remember, spirit is invoked but never commanded.

Magickal uses of the elements

Beyond circle casting, the elements are used in countless ways.

- **Earth** for grounding after spellwork, creating talismans or prosperity magick.
- **Air** for written spells or divination practices.
- **Fire** in candle magick, passion spells or transformation rituals.
- **Water** in ritual baths, blessing jars or scrying bowls.
- **Spirit** in meditation, prayer or to bind intention to the divine.

When we weave the elements into magick, we are not only using symbols but awakening the eternal powers that sustain life. To honour them is to remember that we are both made of and surrounded by these forces, forever part of the balance of existence.

The magickal elements and their correspondences

EARTH

- **The grounding element:** the foundation of life and our anchor
- **Colours:** green, yellow, brown and black
- **Correspondences:** soil, salt, patchouli and oak
- **Elemental spirit:** gnomes
- **Magickal tool:** cauldron, as a vessel of containment for herbs, etc.
- **Magickal uses:** prosperity, abundance, growth and protection
- **Positive qualities:** stability, grounding, responsibility, respect and endurance
- **Negative qualities:** stubbornness, rigidity
- **Cardinal direction:** north
- **Season:** winter
- **Deities:** Mother Earth, nurturing spirit of the planet, embodying fertility, abundance and the cycles of life that sustain all beings

AIR

- **The invisible element:** unseen, but felt all around us
- **Colours:** white, yellow and silver
- **Correspondences:** incense, lavender and feathers
- **Elemental spirit:** sylphs
- **Magickal tool:** athame
- **Magickal uses:** knowledge, divination, creativity and new beginnings
- **Positive qualities:** inspiration, abundance and endurance
- **Negative qualities:** destructive weather, gossiping, forgetfulness
- **Cardinal direction:** east
- **Season:** spring
- **Deities:** Athena, goddess of wisdom, strategy and crafts

FIRE

- **The destructive element:** strong and striking, but also life-sustaining
- **Colours:** red, gold, orange and white
- **Correspondences:** candles, cinnamon and dragons
- **Elemental spirit:** salamanders
- **Magickal tool:** wand
- **Magickal uses:** courage, sexuality, energy and purification
- **Positive qualities:** transformation, health and strength
- **Negative qualities:** hate, jealousy, anger, conflict
- **Cardinal direction:** south
- **Season:** summer
- **Deities:** Brigid, Celtic goddess of fire, healing and poetry

WATER

- **The essential element:** emotions, healing and dreams
- **Colours:** blue, green, indigo and black
- **Correspondences:** seashells, rose and myrrh
- **Elemental spirit:** undines
- **Magickal tool:** chalice
- **Magickal uses:** love, dreams, psychic work and purification
- **Positive qualities:** passion, forgiveness, intuition
- **Negative qualities:** laziness, insecurity, lack of control over emotions
- **Cardinal direction:** west
- **Season:** autumn
- **Deities:** Boann, goddess of the river Boyne in Ireland, linked to wisdom and inspiration

SPIRIT

- » **The ever-present element:** connection and balance
- » **Colours:** white, purple, violet
- » **Magickal tool:** the pentacle
- » *The spirit has no energy type or cardinal direction. It has both positive and negative qualities. It is associated with all seasons and timings.*

Elemental spirits

Elemental spirits are the unseen guardians of nature's forces, the living essences of the elements. They are not bound by flesh and bone, but move in wind, flame, river and stone, guiding and shaping the energies that sustain the world.

Each element has its spirit allies:

- Earth spirits dwell in rock, soil and root, steadying us with their patience and grounding strength.

- Air spirits are carried on every breeze, bringing clarity, inspiration and the spark of new ideas.
- Fire spirits flicker in flame, igniting passion, courage and transformation.
- Water spirits flow through rivers, tides and rain, carrying emotion, healing and intuition.
- And at the centre, spirit itself is the etheric current connecting us to the divine and uniting all other elements.

When we call the elements in ritual, we also invite their spirits to join us. They balance the circle, protect sacred space and infuse our work with living power. To honour elemental spirits is to recognise that magick is never ours alone, but a collaboration with the forces of nature that surround and sustain us.

Earth: Gnomes

Gnomes are the elemental spirits of earth, often imagined as small, sturdy guardians of rock, soil, roots and hidden places. They are the keepers of treasures below the ground, both literal and symbolic: gold, crystals, seeds and the earth's own quiet wisdom.

The term 'gnome' entered European lore in the 16th century through the writings of Paracelsus,, who described them as beings that moved effortlessly through soil and stone. Paracelsus was a Swiss physician, theologian and philosopher who worked extensively on the relationship between nature, the elements and healing.

Spirits of the earth appeared in many traditions long before Paracelsus. In Norse mythology, dwarves were great craftsmen of weapons, jewels and magickal tools and in Celtic tales, the land was alive with fairy folk and nature beings who were guardians of fertility, fields and harvest. Gnomes carry echoes of all these ancestral spirits: those who live below, shaping the unseen foundations of life.

A gnome's presence is steady and grounding, reminding us of patience, responsibility and endurance. In magick, they represent structure and remind us to build carefully in balance with the cycles of nature. In balance, they offer prosperity, endurance and security; out of balance, they can appear as stubbornness, rigidity or resistance to change.

To bring the spirit of gnomes into your practice, leave offerings of soil, stones or crystals and spend time gardening, tending plants or walking barefoot on the land. Face north – the direction of earth – when calling on their presence. Grounding and earthing will also help you connect with their spirit.

EXERCISE: CONNECTING WITH GNOMES

Sit outdoors with a stone or handful of soil. Hold it while thanking the earth for its support. Place an offering – bread, seeds, flowers or crystals – into the ground, asking the gnomes for grounding, stability and prosperity.

Fire: Salamanders

Salamanders are the elemental spirits of fire, the keepers of flame, spark and transformation. Unlike the small amphibian that shares their name, these beings are described in magickal lore as radiant, flickering shapes moving within firelight. Salamanders are tongues of flame given spirit and will. They embody passion, courage, energy and the power of change.

The word 'salamander' first appeared in Paracelsus's alchemical texts, where he identified them as fire elementals. Yet the connection to the element of fire magick runs deeper. In mythology, fire was always alive: the Greeks told of Prometheus stealing fire from the gods, while the Celts revered Brigid as a goddess of flame, hearth and inspiration. The salamander carries these myths within its essence, embodying the divine gift of fire that both destroys and renews.

In magickal practice, salamanders represent the creative and creation spark, the force that ignites new beginnings and fuels transformation. They teach us about courage, willpower and intensity. In balance, salamanders bring inspiration, warmth, vitality and determination. Out of balance, their energy can flare into anger, recklessness or destruction. Like fire itself, they demand respect.

To connect with salamanders, work with flame in mindful ways. Light a candle in ritual, focusing on the dancing flame as a doorway to their presence. Commune with their energy by fire gazing – staring into a hearth, bonfire or candle.

Facing the south, fire's cardinal direction, aligns your practice with their strength. Offerings might include herbs such as rosemary or cinnamon cast into the flame, always with gratitude.

EXERCISE: CONNECTING WITH SALAMANDERS

Light a single candle. As you watch the flame, breathe deeply and visualise your inner fire igniting: your passion, courage and creative spirit are emboldened. Whisper an intention into the flame, asking the salamanders to bless it with energy and transformation.

Air: Sylphs

Sylphs are the elemental spirits of air, subtle and elusive beings that embody breath, wind and the unseen currents that carry thought and inspiration. Sylphs are said to be light, graceful and ever-moving, a breeze dancing across a field or the rustle of wings high above the clouds.

Paracelsus also popularised the term 'sylph' through his writings in the Renaissance, describing them as invisible beings of the air. Yet the idea of airy spirits is far older: Greek mythology spoke of the Anemoi, the four wind gods, and Celtic lore told of spirits that whispered through groves and sacred oaks. Countless traditions equated breath itself with life-force – pneuma, spiritus or prana. Sylphs carry these threads of myth, representing the sacred breath that links body, spirit and sky.

In magickal practice, sylphs are connected to clarity, communication, intellect and imagination. They bring sudden insights, inspiration and the ability to see situations with fresh perspective. When balanced, they foster curiosity, adaptability and vision. When unbalanced, they may manifest as restlessness, overthinking or detachment.

To connect with sylphs, seek out places where the air is alive – hilltops, breezy meadows or forests where leaves are stirred by wind. Facing east, the cardinal direction of air, aligns you with their realm, as does working at dawn, the time of new breath. Feathers, incense and bells are offerings and tools often associated with sylph energy.

EXERCISE: CONNECTING WITH SYLPHS

Step outdoors on a breezy day. Close your eyes and feel the air moving across your skin. Breathe deeply, imagining sylphs riding the currents around you.

Whisper a question or intention into the wind, trusting the sylphs to carry it into the wider universe and return with clarity.

Water: Undines

Undines are the elemental spirits of water, graceful beings that dwell in rivers, lakes, seas and springs. They embody the qualities of emotion, intuition, adaptability and healing. Just as water can soothe, cleanse and nourish, undines remind us of the depth of feeling and the flow of life's currents.

Again, although popularised by Paracelsus's writings, water spirits have appeared in myth across many cultures since time immemorial. In ancient Greek lore, the Nereids were sea nymphs, daughters of Nereus, who guided sailors and represented the beauty and danger of the sea. In Japanese Shinto tradition, certain kami are spirits of rivers, waterfalls and rain, honoured for bringing fertility and purification. These traditions reflect the reverence for water as both giver and taker of life, an element to be respected and honoured.

Undines are often imagined as mermaid-like figures or translucent beings who rise with the mist, guiding dreams and emotions. They govern the tides of our inner world, encouraging compassion, empathy and sensitivity. In balance, they help us connect with love, creativity and intuition. Out of balance, their influence may manifest as moodiness, over-sensitivity or the feeling of drowning in emotion.

To connect with undines, seek water in its natural forms. Visit the sea, walk by a river or sit beside a fountain. Face west to align your practice with their realm. Use shells, bowls of water or silver chalices on your altar as offerings, or pour a little water onto the ground as a gesture of respect.

EXERCISE: CONNECTING WITH UNDINES

Sit beside a body of water or place a bowl of water before you. Dip your fingers into it, close your eyes, and ask the undines to cleanse away stagnant emotion. Whisper your intention, imagining it flowing into the water to be carried onward.

CHAPTER 7

Magick throughout the year

The wheel turns, and with it the
song of the earth changes.

From the stillness of winter's hush to the
bright laughter of spring, from summer's
fiery embrace to autumn's golden release, each
season carries a voice, a lesson, a gift.

They remind us that nothing stays the same.

Rest is sacred, growth inevitable, harvest is
a blessing, and endings are a promise of renewal.

To walk the witch's path is to walk in rhythm
with these ancient tides, to feel the pulse of
the land within your own heartbeat and
to honour the cycles that shape all life.

The Wheel of the Year is the magickal term for the Wiccan calendar, a sacred cycle that honours the turning of the seasons and the earth's continual rotation around the sun. The wheel reflects a cyclical understanding of life – birth, growth, death and renewal. By attuning to these seasonal rhythms, witches align their practice with the natural flow of the universe.

The Wheel of the Year is made up of eight festivals, known as sabbats. Four are 'solar festivals', governed by the sun's movement. These are the two solstices and equinoxes, when light and darkness shift in balance. The remaining four festivals are called 'fire festivals' after ancient Celtic tradition. These mark agricultural milestones such as sowing, harvest and winter survival. Together the eight festivals, or significant points in the cycle, form a wheel – a continuous journey through light and dark, death and rebirth.

Historically, many of these celebrations were drawn from Celtic and Germanic pagan practices that honoured the land and its cycles of fertility. Samhain, the Celtic new year, was a time to honour ancestors, while Beltane was a bonfire festival celebrating fertility and union.

Wicca, emerging in the mid-20th century through the work of Gerald Gardner and others, wove these ancient traditions into a unified cycle, giving modern witches a framework to celebrate nature's sacred turning. Each date is celebrated with unique rituals and is considered particularly potent for specific forms of magick: Yule for rebirth, Imbolc for purification, Ostara for growth, Litha for power, Lughnasadh for abundance, Mabon for balance, Samhain for transformation and Beltane for passion.

By walking the Wheel of the Year, witches are reminded that they, too, are part of nature's cycles. To celebrate these turning points is to live in harmony with the earth and to weave magick into the seasons themselves.

The southern hemisphere

If you are practicing in the southern hemisphere, the Wheel of the Year is best adopted by following the local seasons rather than fixed calendar dates. This usually means shifting the festivals by approximately six months so that seasonal energies – such as growth, harvest and rest – are aligned with what is happening in the natural world around you. For example, festivals associated with mid-winter or the return of the light are typically celebrated around June in the southern hemisphere rather than December.

SAMHAIN

ALL HALLOWS EVE, HALLOWEEN
31ST OCTOBER

Samhain is a preparation for the God's retreat into the shadows of winter. Night comes to dominate the day as the third and final harvest of the year is complete. Traditionally, Pagans of old left food for their ancestors. Faces were carved on root vegetables and candles placed inside them to guide spirits visiting this realm.

Things to do:

- Set a place at the dinner table for the dead.
- Light a candle to guide ancestral spirits.
- Leave offerings of bread, apples or drink.
- Light a bonfire for protection and blessing.

Correspondences:

- **Crystals:** obsidian, onyx, jet
- **Trees:** oak, elder, apple
- **Colours:** black, silver, orange

YULE

WINTER SOLSTICE
20TH–23RD DECEMBER

Yule is a festive holiday of light taking place in the depths of winter. It is a time for quiet reflection, inner focus and rest, and traditionally celebrated by gathering for feasts and giving symbolic gifts that represent light, protection and goodwill to be carried into the new cycle.

Things to do:

» Decorate a Yule tree.
» Make a wreath.
» Have a bonfire.
» Reap the benefits of the growing season by making food with seasonal vegetables.

Correspondences:

» **Crystals:** clear quartz, garnet, obsidian
» **Trees:** mistletoe, ivy, holly
» **Colours:** green, gold, brown

IMBOLC

CANDLEMAS, ST. BRIGID'S DAY
1ST–2ND FEBRUARY

Imbolc is a time for awakening after a long slumber. Rituals begin after the inactivity of the long winter, often with the intention of planting future seeds. Imbolc is associated with beginnings and growth, and it is known as the 'festival of the maiden' in modern Pagan practice.

Things to do:

» Plant seeds.
» Perform a cleansing and blessing ritual.
» Perform an awakening ritual.
» Give thanks for the light.

Correspondences:

» **Crystals:** amethyst, moonstone, citrine
» **Trees:** birch, rowan, hazel
» **Colours:** white, soft green, pale yellow

OSTARA

SPRING EQUINOX
20TH–23RD MARCH

Ostara is a festival of growth and rising energy. Gardening begins as the natural world begins to bloom. Equal day and night brings balance and opposing forces into harmony.

Things to do:

» Paint decorative eggs.
» Bake bread and hot cross buns.
» Plant and nurture seeds of your spiritual garden.

Correspondences:

» **Crystals:** rose quartz, fluorite, green aventurine
» **Trees:** apple, alder, ash
» **Colours:** pink, yellow, sky blue

BELTANE

MAY DAY
1ST MAY

As spring moves into summer, a fire festival is held at Beltane. Fertility is at its height and the earth begins to flourish with new life.

Things to do:

» Visit a holy well, fairy fort or stone circle.
» Light a bonfire.
» Make flower crowns.

Correspondences:

» **Crystals:** emerald, carnelian, rose quartz
» **Trees:** may blossom, hawthorn, rowan
» **Colours:** red, pink, white

LITHA

SUMMER SOLSTICE, MIDSUMMER
20TH–23RD JUNE

At Litha, the God and Goddess are at the peak of their power and the sun is at its highest point. It is often considered the most magickal time of the year and is a time of celebration and rest before the work of the harvest.

Things to do:

» Hold a solstice feast.
» Hold a bonfire gathering.
» Celebrate the abundance of light and warmth.

Correspondences:

» **Crystals:** sunstone, tiger's eye, clear quartz
» **Trees:** oak, elder, ash
» **Colours:** gold, yellow, blue

LUGHNASADH

LAMMAS
1ST AUGUST

The first of three harvest festivals, Lughnasadh is a time to give thanks for the abundance of the growing season and the work of the harvest. Kitchen witchery is popular at this time and it is customary to bless freshly made loaves of bread.

Things to do:

» Meditate.
» Go berry picking.
» Divination rituals.
» Prepare a garden-to-table meal.
» Bake fresh bread.

Correspondences:

» **Crystals:** peridot, jasper, tiger's eye
» **Trees:** birch, rowan, hazel
» **Colours:** brown, orange, green

MABON

AUTUMN EQUINOX
20TH–23RD SEPTEMBER

At Mabon, preparations begin for the coming winter and the God's approaching mythical death at Samhain. Equal days and nights mean balance is the theme of this second harvest.

Things to do:

» Harvest the fruits of your physical and metaphysical garden.

» Decorate your altar.

» Give thanks.

» Spend time outdoors.

Correspondences:

» **Crystals:** agate, carnelian, smoky quartz

» **Trees:** maple, vine, apple

» **Colours:** orange, brown, green

Seasonal magick

The seasons are the heartbeat of the earth. Each brings its own energy, a current that can be harnessed in spellwork, ritual and intention.

Witches may plant a spell of growth in spring, kindle passion in summer, release in autumn and rest in winter. When we honour the turning seasons, we honour the cycles within ourselves: our own growth, fullness, decline and renewal. In this way, the seasons are a pillar of magick, guiding the festivals and rituals that weave our practice into the rhythm of the earth itself.

- **Samhain** marks the end of the harvest and the honouring of ancestors. It is known as the start of the new year in many Celtic and Pagan traditions.
- **Yule** celebrates the rebirth of the sun in the darkest days.
- **Imbolc** brings the first stirrings of spring, a time of purification and blessing.
- **Ostara** welcomes balance, fertility and new growth.
- **Beltane** is a festival of passion, fire, creativity and union.
- **Litha** honours the sun at its height.
- **Lughnasadh** celebrates the first harvest, a time of gratitude and abundance.
- **Mabon** marks balance once more, as the light and dark of the year meet.

By attuning ourselves to these turning points, we come into deeper alignment with the earth. We remember that we, too, have seasons – times of growth, times of rest, times of letting go and times of renewal.

CHAPTER 8

Nature's magickal tools

In quiet gardens healing hides,
soft leaves where ancient magick bides,
a sprig of sage, mint's cool sigh,
balm for the heart and the wandering eye.

Rosemary hums of memory's song,
thyme keeps courage steady and strong.

Each stem a spell, each root a prayer.

Nature's own wisdom woven with care.

Herbs are among the oldest tools of magick. To work with herbs is to step into a tradition as ancient as the first healers and wise ones, who looked to the hedgerow, forest and field for remedies and charms.

Each plant holds its own energy, a unique vibration shaped by sun, soil and season. When we bring herbs into magickal practice, we are partnering with these natural allies and working with their specific energies, weaving their power with our own intention.

Herbs are tangible vessels of energy: the living spirit of the earth itself is carried within their leaves, roots and flowers. The very scent, texture or taste of a herb carries memory and meaning. They awaken the subconscious and amplify intention, grounding our practice in the cycles of the earth.

Herbs for witchcraft

There are many ways to work with herbs in magick. Dried herbs can be burned as incense or scattered in circles for protection. Teas and infusions allow their energy to be taken internally, blending body and spirit. Herbs can be added to charm bags, herbal pouches or spell bottles to attract specific energies. Or you can carry them on your person in a pocket, locket or sewn into clothing as quiet companions throughout the day.

Herbs are also often used for cleansing and clearing energy, with white sage (for cleansing and purification) and palo santo (for sweetening and refreshing energy) being the most popular. When using each, a small amount is sufficient with the focus being on intention.

In every form, herbs remind us that magick need not be distant or abstract. It grows in gardens, along roadsides and in the quiet corners of nature. To honour the power of herbs is to remember that the earth is alive and always willing to lend her gifts to those who listen.

In Chapter 11, we will look more closely at which herbs are best suited for different kinds of spells – from love and abundance to protection, healing and divination – so you can begin building your own herbal practice with confidence and intention.

Lavender *(Lavandula angustifolia)*

Lavender is one of the most beloved herbs in magickal and healing traditions, known for its calming scent and soothing presence. With soft purple flowers and gentle fragrance, lavender carries the energy of peace, purification and protection.

In folklore, sprigs of lavender were hung in homes to ward off evil spirits, burned to cleanse a space or carried as charms for love and luck. It is also deeply connected to the element of air and often used in dreamwork, meditation and spells of serenity.

Lavender is versatile in magickal practice. Dried flowers can be placed in charm bags or sachets to invite rest and sweet dreams. Infusions or teas calm the spirit, while incense made with lavender clears the air of heavy energy. Sprinkled in a ritual bath, it softens the heart and prepares the mind for deeper spiritual work.

One of my favourite personal experiences with lavender came during a period of high stress, when sleepless nights made everything feel heavier. I filled a small pouch with dried lavender, added a few drops of lavender oil and placed it under my pillow. That night I fell into the most restful sleep I had experienced in weeks, waking with a renewed sense of calm and clarity. It reminded me how powerful herbs can be when used with intention, not only to shift energy but to restore balance within ourselves. For me, lavender is more than a herb. It is a trusted companion, a reminder that peace is always within reach, and that nature's simplest gifts often carry the deepest magick.

Gathering and drying fresh herbs

Working with herbs begins with preparation. Treat each step as a ritual in itself, honouring the plant's spirit as much as its form. If you can, use fresh herbs in magickal workings, from your own garden if you have one. But use what you have available!

- Gather fresh herbs ideally on a dry morning, after the morning dew has dried.

- Follow the rules of: *Leave the first, leave the last and take only what serves you.*

To prevent fresh herbs from going mouldy, dry them out completely. Tie small bundles with natural twine and hang them upside down in a warm, airy place away from direct sunlight. Once they are dry and crisp, store them in glass jars, labelled with their name and the date.

Maceration

Maceration is a simple way of drawing the properties of herbs and plants into a liquid by letting them steep in liquid over time. It is an old, reliable method used to create herbal oils, teas, tinctures and vinegars. In ritual craft, maceration is also an 'infusion' process, ideal when you want your intention to build gradually and steadily.

1. **Prepare your ingredients and vessel.** Select your herb after drying. Choose a suitable glass jar. It should be clean and dry with a tight-fitting lid.
2. **Fill the jar.** Fill the jar half full (loosely packed) with your dried herb.
3. **Add your oil.** Cover the herbs completely with oil, leaving 1–2cm of space at the top. Suitable oils to use are sunflower or grapeseed.
4. **Label.** Include the herb name, oil, date and intended use.
5. **Steep and leave.** Store in a cool, dark place for 2–6 weeks. (For oils usually 2–4 weeks is sufficient.)
6. **Shake daily.** This will help with extraction and prevent clumping.

7. **Strain.** Once ready, use muslin, cotton or a paper coffee filter to strain. Squeeze well.
8. **Bottle and store.** Decant into a clean dark bottle and label with date, name and intended use.

Herbal tinctures

A herbal tincture captures the essence of a herb in liquid form, this time using alcohol. Tinctures can be used in spellwork, anointing candles or as drops in ritual water (**not for consumption!**).

1. Half-fill a small glass jar with chopped fresh or dried herbs. Cover completely with an alcohol (such as vodka) and seal.
2. Place the jar in a cool, dark spot for 2–4 weeks. During this time, you may choose to gently shake the jar every few days and focus on your intention for the tincture.
3. Strain through muslin, bottle and label. Store in a cool, dark place.

Herbal teas

Herbal teas have been used for both medicinal and spiritual purposes all around the world for centuries. The ancient Egyptians, traditional Chinese medicine practitioners, Celtic healers and wise women of Europe were all known to use infusions of leaves, flowers and roots to soothe the body, strengthen the spirit and open the mind to deeper awareness.

Spiritually, teas are more than simple drinks – they are potions crafted with intention. When brewed thoughtfully, each cup becomes a ritual in itself, blending the healing essence of herbs with the energy of water, an element of intuition and flow.

The act of preparing tea – selecting herbs, boiling water, inhaling the rising steam, taking the first sip – can calm the mind, ground the body and create sacred space.

Herbal teas are especially powerful in magickal practice because they allow us to take the energy of plants into ourselves. For example, chamomile brings peace and sleep, peppermint sharpens focus, rose softens the heart and mugwort is used for dreaming and divination. Drinking such teas before meditation, spellwork or prayer prepares the spirit to receive, relax and open.

Teas can also be used to set intentions. As you sip, focus on your desire – abundance, healing, clarity – and imagine the herb's energy filling you with that purpose. A simple cup of tea becomes a spell in motion, working from within.

Whether taken for health, ritual, or quiet reflection, herbal teas connect us to the ancient tradition of plant magick, reminding us that every sip is an offering of the earth.

Common teas and their magickal properties

- **Calendula:** soothes raw feelings and helps you feel 'put back together'.
- **Chamomile:** associated with rest, deep sleep and peaceful dreams.
- **Green:** gently cleanses stagnant energy and scattered thinking.
- **Lavender:** offers serenity and protection.
- **Licorice:** helps seal energy leaks caused by stress.

- **Mint:** lifts burdens and eases the breath after a heavy day.
- **Valerian:** calms anxiety that lives in the physical body.

Note: Valerian is a strong herb. Use occasionally and preferably in the evening as it may cause drowsiness. Do not combine with alcohol or sedatives.

EXERCISE: A MAGICKAL TEA CEREMONY

Tea is more than a drink: it is a sacred act. In Japan, the *chanoyu* or tea ceremony evolved into a spiritual practice of mindfulness and respect, where every movement was intentional and infused with beauty. In China, offering tea to guests was a gesture of harmony and honour. Even in Celtic and European folk traditions, herbal infusions were shared as medicine and blessing, marking community and ritual.

The importance of the tea ceremony lies in its simplicity: an ordinary act transformed into a ritual. By slowing down, honouring the herbs and drinking with awareness, we connect to the timeless traditions of those who came before us. Tea becomes more than refreshment. It is a meditation, an offering and a spell all in one.

To create your own magickal tea ceremony, you do not need elaborate tools – only tea and your intention.

You will need:

- Your tea of choice or a small handful of herbs (chamomile, rose, lavender or any blend chosen for your purpose)
- Recently boiled hot water
- A simple cup or teapot
- Optional: candles, crystals or a small cloth to turn your table into an altar.

Instructions:

1. Before you begin, pause, set down the noise of the day and return to yourself.
2. Holding the herbs in your hands, focus on your intention: peace, healing, clarity or love.
3. Ready the herbs in the teapot or cup. As you pour the hot water over the herbs, visualise their energy infusing the liquid with your desire. When the steam rises, inhale deeply, letting the fragrance open your senses. *Please exercise caution when using hot water.*
4. Sip slowly, as though each mouthful were a blessing. Between sips, pause in silence. This is communing with the earth and with your spirit.
5. Send gratitude to the herbs and the earth for their support. Give thanks for the soil that nourished this plant, the rain that fed it and the sun that warmed it.
6. After the ceremony, write a few lines in your journal about what you noticed between sips: the sensations, thoughts and moments of stillness. Let the words flow without trying to analyse or identify anything.

The magick of trees

'Trees are sanctuaries. Whoever knows how to speak to them, whoever knows how to listen to them, can learn the truth.'

–Hermann Hesse, *Wandering: Notes and Sketches*, 1920

As we saw in chapter five, spending time among trees has always held a kind of enchantment. The forest nourishes not only our spirit but our nervous system. Beyond this, trees carry deep spiritual significance.

Quietly growing strong over the centuries, trees are the living embodiment of rootedness. They represent the cycles of life and death that continue regardless of human haste. To walk amongst the trees is to remember we are part of something vast and enduring, far bigger than our own concerns.

When I need an escape from the hustle and bustle of life, I step into the forest and my world shifts. The air grows cooler, carrying the scent of damp earth and moss. The light softens as it filters through the canopy, dappling the ground in shades of green and gold.

With each breath, each step crunching softly over fallen leaves, I feel something uncoil inside me – a tension I hadn't realised I was holding. The deeper I walk, the more alive I feel. It is as if the trees themselves are humming in a low vibration beneath the silence, steady and grounding. I always reach out to touch the bark of an ancient oak, its rough skin warm under my palm, and for a moment it feels as though I am greeting an old friend. My chest loosens, my thoughts clear and my energy begins to flow again where it has been stagnant.

Have you noticed how cool the air becomes beneath a forest canopy? That shift is not only physical but spiritual, a reminder of nature's embrace. In those shaded paths, where silence hums with life, we are reminded of our connection – in body, mind and spirit – to the living world.

Tree spirits: the keepers of balance

Once upon an Irish time, trees ruled the land, stretching their limbs across hills and valleys, and covering nearly 80 per cent of the country in vast, whispering forests. To our ancestors, these trees were more than wood and leaf: they were guardians, storytellers and living beings infused with sacred power.

Though much of that forest has long since vanished, felled for survival and settlement, their aura lingers still, shimmering with enchantment and carrying echoes of the ancient magick that once was so deeply rooted in this land. Within those echoes dwell the guardians of the trees: the Green Man, the Holly King and the Oak King and countless other nature spirits who embody the cycles of growth, death and renewal.

The Green Man, his face carved in leaves and vines, is the eternal spirit of vegetation and rebirth. He reminds us that every season brings renewal and that life returns even after the darkest winter. The Holly King and the Oak King rule over half the year each, meeting in a mythical battle at each equinox to mark the shifting of the seasons. These figures are not distant gods but personifications of the natural cycles that govern the earth – growth and decay, light and dark, endings and beginnings.

In magickal practice, such spirits serve as bridges between human and nature. By invoking the Green Man, a witch may draw strength for fertility, creativity and new ventures. By working with the Holly King, one might honour release, endings or protection during the darker months. These guardians embody the very energies practitioners seek to align with, making them powerful allies in ritual.

Nature spirits remind us of our place in the greater whole, the unseen keepers of balance. They are the energies that flow through river, stone and tree. To honour them is to acknowledge that magick does not come from us alone, but from the living world around us. When we work with nature spirits, we are not commanding forces but collaborating with them, entering into a relationship of respect and reciprocity. The trees may no longer cover Ireland as they once did, but their spirits endure, guardians of a forgotten forest still whispering to those who listen.

The Green Man

Behold the mystical being known as the Green Man, harbinger of change in the verdant realm. He embodies the spirit of the plants, trees and foliage, and he is a conductor of their magick. His essence weaves through the very fabric of growth and rebirth, ushering in the dawn of spring. When you gaze upon his visage, you witness the enchantment of nature's bounty.

The Oak King

As the wheel of the year spins, the Oak King emerges in his verdant glory, heralding the season of growth and summer's warmth. The Oak King is at his greatest strength at the summer solstice. The wise Celts bestowed upon him this name and considered him to be an embodiment of vitality and renewal. He reigns supreme over his counterpart, the Holly King, until the balance of the autumn equinox tips the scales in the other's favour.

The Holly King

As the vibrant leaves turn to rust and gold, the Holly King ascends to claim the throne of his counterpart, the Oak King. The Holly King reigns over the dwindling days and colder months, peaking in strength in midwinter. He holds sway until the dawn of Ostara, when the Oak King is restored and the world blooms anew.

EXERCISE: HONOURING THE TREE SPIRITS

- Begin with permission. Before touching, gathering or sitting beneath a tree, pause. Place a hand on its trunk and quietly ask for permission.
- Offer, don't take. Simple offerings are best: clean water poured at the roots, a song or a few spoken words of thanks, or a pinch of oats, bread or seeds.

- Speak aloud from the heart. Tree spirits respond to presence more than poetry. Say why you are there.
- Sit and listen. Time is the true offering. Sit quietly against the trunk or near the roots. Let your breathing slow. Notice sensations, thoughts or images without forcing meaning.
- Return to the same tree throughout the year, honouring bud, leaf, fruit and bare branch. Acknowledging these changes honours the tree's cycle and deepens your relationship with it.

EXERCISE: RITUAL OF THE TREE SPIRITS

Connect with the Oak King, the Holly King and the Green Man to recognise where you are in the cycle of growth, release and renewal.

Use this ritual any time of the year. The spirits are not fixed to dates: they move through us as states of being. There are no 'right' answers here. Awareness is the work.

You will need:

- Images or items to represent each tree spirit: an acorn or oak leaf, a holly berry or leaf, and sprig of wood
- A candle and a lighter or matches
- Journal and pen

Instructions:

1. Take a breath and place the three representations in front of you. Light the candle and say '*I honour the turning of the year and the spirits that move through it.*'
2. Call the spirits, quietly, one at a time. Pause after each incantation. Do not rush.

    Oak King – Spirit of the waxing light
    Place your hand on the representation of the oak and say:
    '*Oak King, guide of growth and strength, show me where I am called to expand.*'

    Holly King – Spirit of the waning light
    Place your hand on the representation of the holly and say:
    '*Holly King, keeper of rest and release, show me what I am ready to let go of.*'

    Green Man – Spirit of life force and renewal
    Touch the symbol of the Green Man and say:
    '*Green Man, breath of the living land, show me how life wishes to move through me.*'

3. Sit in stillness for 3–5 minutes. Notice which symbol draws your attention most. This is the spirit currently active in your life.
4. In your journal, write under each heading what stood out.

    Oak King
    Where am I being asked to grow or step forward?
    What strength is emerging in me right now?

Holly King
What needs to rest, end or be released?
Where am I holding on to something past its season?

Green Man
Where does life want to flow more freely through me?
What would renewal look like if I trusted it?

5. Close the practice by saying:
   '*I honour the cycle and my place within it.*' Extinguish the candle.

The magick of crystals

Crystals are believed to have unique energetic properties that can be used to assist in healing, enhancing intentions, manifestation and spellwork. The use of crystals has a long history and across many cultures. Not just purely decorative, stones were often chosen intentionally based on tradition, symbolism or personal need, and they were believed to act as a companion during times of challenge, transition or intention setting. High-ranking officers in ancient Rome would sometimes wear amulets or helmets with decorated crystals when going into battle. Cleopatra used ground lapis lazuli as an eyeshadow – although I do not recommend doing this today!

Today, lapis lazuli is associated with wisdom, truth and clear communication. It is often used to support self-expression and honest speech, and to encourage confidence in matters of communication. It is also linked with the mind and inner vision, making it a common choice for divination practices.

In modern magickal practice, witches will carry crystals as personal talismans, incorporate them into spellwork, place them on their altar, or use them during meditation to support focus. Some common uses for crystals as spiritual support are:

- Attracting love, self-love and emotional support
- Reproductive health and fertility
- Protection from negative energy
- Assisting in focus during meditation
- Grounding.

Cleansing crystals

Crystals are powerful allies, but they absorb the energies they encounter like sponges in water. To keep the vibration of a crystal clear and strong, it should be energetically cleansed regularly. This ensures the crystal remains attuned to your highest intentions and is not retaining stagnant or negative energy. Cleansing is not only care for the crystal, it is also a ritual of respect for the partnership you share.

There are many ways to cleanse crystals. Trust your intuition and choose the one that feels most natural to you. Here are some common ways:

- Meditate with your crystals, visualising the negative energy being removed.
- Smudge with palo santo or sage.
- Place crystals under moonlight, preferably on a full moon.
- Hold under running water.

- Place crystals in sunlight to use the heat of the sun to cleanse them.
- Bury crystals in the earth overnight to allow them to soak up grounding energy.

Note: Thoroughly research the properties of your crystals before choosing one of these options. Quartz could be a fire hazard in sunlight because of its magnifying properties; some crystals will dissolve in water, such as selenite.

Crystals and their magickal properties

- **Tiger's eye:** alleviates depression, balances yin and yang energies, encourages prosperity, lifts mood, energises the emotional body and brings abundance.
- **Citrine:** attracts abundance and prosperity, supports healing after trauma, eliminates toxins in the lower chakras and disperses congestion in the auric field.
- **Amethyst**: a stone of transformation, calming and stimulating, extremely protective and dispels anger, fear and anxiety.
- **Black obsidian:** grounds and protects, promotes spontaneity, offers comfort, provides protection and promotes forgiveness.
- **Clear quartz:** the 'master healer' crystal. It stores and regulates energy and harmonises all the chakras.

DID YOU KNOW?

CRYSTALS THROUGHOUT THE WHEEL OF THE YEAR

Samhain

With the veil thinning, citrine offers warm resilience and steady illumination in the face of transition. It supports the release of what has passed and encourages the quiet strength needed to embrace endings.

Yule

Garnet and amethyst reflect the deep stillness of midwinter offering protection, endurance and inner clarity for the darkest time of the year. They guard vitality, keep strength alive and sustain spiritual focus until the light begins its slow return. Turquoise also carries protective and restorative qualities for this restful time of the year.

Imbolc

As the first stirrings of renewal emerge, aquamarine offers a cleansing flow of watery energy. It supports internal clarity and represents awakening and quiet preparation for future momentum.

Ostara

Diamond speaks to balance, truth and the sharpening of intention as light and dark stand in harmony at this turning point of the year. The diamond brings clarity of purpose and strengthens new growth.

Beltane

The fertile abundance of late spring is echoed in emerald and moonstone, which have been long linked with growth, creativity and the mysteries of life. Unfolding together they support expansion, intuition and the flowering of ideas and relationships.

Litha

At the height of the sun's power, ruby and peridot embody vitality, confidence and life force. These stones resonate with courage, joy and the sustaining fire of summer.

Lughnasadh

As the first harvest approaches, lapis lazuli brings wisdom, insight and reflection. It supports the integration of experience and the recognition of skills and knowledge gathered during the previous year.

Mabon

Opal reflects the changing light of early autumn. It is associated with balance and emotional awareness, supporting reflection and review as the year moves from this moment of equal day and night towards darker days.

EXERCISE: WHAT IS YOUR FAVOURITE CRYSTAL?

How could the crystal you have selected be beneficial for you?

What enchanted crystals would you like to weave into your rituals? Write them here along with their magickal properties.

How to use magickal crystals

Charging crystals

Crystals are often understood as tools that hold and reflect intention. Charging a crystal is simply the act of consciously aligning it with a purpose before use. There is no single correct method; what matters is clarity and consistency rather than ceremony.

A simple approach is to hold the crystal in your hands, take a few slow breaths, and state your intention clearly either aloud or silently. This might be a single word – such as '*protection*' or '*focus*' – or a short sentence that reflects what you are working towards.

Spelling a crystal

Some people prefer to 'spell' a crystal by infusing it with an intention and spell. This might include placing it upon an altar, beside a candle or inside a herbal pouch overnight. Others choose to work with nature's cycles, leaving crystals in moonlight or daylight as a way of marking a beginning. These actions do not give the crystal added power, so much as they help anchor your intention in the physical world. If none of these methods resonates, simply using the crystal regularly and mindfully is enough. Repetition builds relationships.

Using crystals in daily or ritual practice

Crystals may be placed on an altar, carried in a pocket, used in meditation or included in ritual work alongside herbs, candles or written intentions. When not in use, storing them with care in a cloth or small bowl can help maintain a sense of respect and continuity.

It is helpful to periodically pause and reflect on whether a crystal still feels aligned with its original purpose. If not, it can be gently cleansed and rested until it is needed again.

EXERCISE: WORKING WITH CRYSTALS AND INTENTION

Use this exercise to close the chapter and integrate what you have learned.

1. Choose one crystal you feel drawn to today.
2. Write its name at the top of the page.
3. Answer the following promptly and without overthinking:

   What draws me to this crystal right now?
   What do I need support with in my life right now?
   How do I want to feel when I work with this crystal?
   Where could I place or use this crystal so it becomes part of my daily rhythm?

4. To close, write a single sentence that begins with:
   As I work with this crystal, I commit to:

____

____

____

____

There is no need to force belief or expectation. The purpose of this exercise is awareness – bringing in intention and giving it a place to land within yourself.

CHAPTER 9

Magickal spaces and symbols

Behold the magickal space: a threshold
between the ordinary and the sacred.

Here lies energy like a breath before a word,
alive in candle flame and the shadow of chosen objects,
in symbols that listen as much as they speak,
where stillness holds the answers we quietly seek.

A magickal space is a threshold between the ordinary and the sacred, a place where energy is raised, intention is focused and the unseen becomes tangible. It is a container for your practice in the form of an energetic circle drawn around you and the tools you use. When you step into magickal space, it marks the moment as sacred and distinct from everyday life.

Creating a magickal space doesn't always require elaborate tools or a permanent altar. Rather, it's about cultivating an environment that helps you shift your awareness. This can be as simple as a quiet corner with a candle, a windowsill holding a crystal or plant or even a temporary circle traced outdoors in the dirt. What matters is not how grand it looks, but how it feels to you.

Why is it important to have a dedicated space for rituals and spellcasting? A magickal space acts as an anchor for your energy and intention. When you return to the same spot, your mind and spirit recognise it as sacred ground, making it easier to step into a focused, receptive state.

Over time, the energy you've raised in a magickal space lingers, creating an atmosphere that supports your practice and magnifies your workings. A dedicated space also becomes a reflection of your inner world. The items you place – a feather, a bowl of water, a beloved stone or a symbol of your path – remind you of your connection to the natural cycles and to your own power. Whether permanent or temporary, a magickal space invites you to pause, breathe and engage with mystery. It is a reminder that magick is not distant or abstract but alive in the very places where you stand.

Altars

At your altar you lay down your intentions like seeds and offer whispers of gratitude to your ancestors. There, you return to the stillness of your own spirit. It is a sacred threshold, a meeting ground of earth and sky, nature and spirit. Within its circle, growth unfolds – not only of magick, but of the soul itself.

Altars can be permanent or temporary, each carrying its own gifts and flexibility, and both are equally valid in magickal practice. Permanent magickal spaces are those you return to again and again. An altar in your home is the most common form: it might be a table, shelf or even a small box dedicated to your tools, symbols and offerings. This space grows with you, becoming a touchstone that immediately helps you drop into a ritual mindset.

My own altar sits in a quiet corner of my home. It is adorned with candles, crystals and herbs that change with the seasons, alongside tools such as my cauldron and ritual bowl. Over time, the space has become so charged with energy that simply lighting a candle there feels like stepping into sacred ground.

Temporary magickal spaces, on the other hand, are created when and where they are needed. Not everyone has the privacy, space or desire for a permanent altar. In these cases, a cloth can be laid out, a circle can be cast, or a small arrangement of items can be gathered for the duration of the ritual and then put away. Temporary spaces are especially useful outdoors, where the natural world becomes your altar – a fallen log for your tools, a ring of stones to mark your circle or even the sky above as your canopy.

What matters is not the scale or permanence but the intention behind them. A candle lit in devotion on a kitchen counter can be just as powerful as an elaborately decorated altar that is never used.

By creating and tending to these spaces we carve out room for magick in daily life. In a world full of noise and distraction, stepping into your magickal space signals to your spirit that it is time to focus, connect and create. Over time, you will find that these spaces become sanctuaries, places where you feel safe, aligned and empowered.

Ultimately, whether you choose a permanent altar, a portable pouch of tools, or the openness of a forest clearing, your magickal space will become a mirror of your own practice. It is where intention meets action, and where the everyday world gives way to the sacred.

Creating your own altar

An altar can be as simple or elaborate as you choose, but there are a few practical considerations that can help you create a space that feels both powerful and personal.

Location

Begin by finding a place where you feel comfortable and won't be disturbed. This might be a quiet corner of a bedroom, by a window for natural light, or even a small table or shelf that can be dedicated to spiritual work. Outdoors, it could be in a garden or groves, or by a body of water for seasonal rituals. If privacy is an issue, a box or tray that can be set up and put away works just as well. The key is choosing a space where you feel safe, calm and able to focus.

Permanent or temporary

Decide whether your altar will be permanent or temporary. A permanent altar is left in place and becomes a constant reminder of your spiritual path. It will hold the energy of repeated rituals, making it a potent anchor. A temporary altar is created only when needed, then dismantled and packed away. This option is ideal for those with limited space or who wish to keep their practice private. Neither is better – what matters is what suits your life and practice.

Placement

Traditionally, altars are aligned with the cardinal directions, especially east (associated with air and inspiration) or north (earth and grounding). However, you may choose any direction that feels right.

Decoration

Add anything to an altar that resonates with you. This may include candles, crystals, a bowl of water, incense and symbols of the four elements. Many witches also include a representation of divinity, such as a goddess or god figure, a photo of ancestors or a natural item like a shell or stone. You may also add your personal tools, such as a wand, athame or tarot deck. Arrange them in a way that feels balanced, perhaps with elemental items arranged to face their corresponding directions: earth to the north, air to the east, fire to the south and water to the west.

Why it matters

Setting up your altar is never about perfection; it's about creating a space where your magick feels alive. Whether permanent or temporary, simple or ornate, your altar becomes a focal point for your practice. It is a place where intention is nurtured, where the veil thins and where the sacred meets the mundane.

Altar inspiration

Some common magickal tools and symbols for altars are:

- A pentagram for protection, balance and unity.
- Herbs for healing, protection and wisdom.
- A crystal ball for insight, divination and clarity. (*Be careful never to leave crystal balls uncovered in sunlight, as they may light a fire.*)
- Anointing oil for blessing, power and intention.
- Tarot for guidance, insight and reflection.
- Representation/s of the gods and/or goddesses of creation, nurture and wisdom.
- Incense for purification, prayer and focus.
- Candles for light, intention and transformation.

- Crystals for energy, power and healing.
- Flowers or house plants for grounding, beauty and connection to the natural world.

What drives you to seek solace at your altar? Write it in the frame.

Cleansing your magickal space

It is important to cleanse your home and altar before undertaking any magickal work. It's also great to do a space cleanse more generally if you perceive there is any negative energy in your home.

Cleansing creates a clear receptive foundation much like sweeping a floor before laying down a ritual cloth. It is not about fear, superstition or the idea that something is *wrong*. Rather, it is about resetting energy, establishing intention and marking the transition from the ordinary into the sacred.

Cleansing is also valuable outside of ritual context. Homes hold energy. They absorb stress, arguments, illness, grief, exhaustion and even the residue of visitors passing through. It may be time for a gentle cleanse if you perceive heaviness, have disrupted sleep or are struggling with irritability – or if you just have a general sense that a space feels off.

Cleanse…

- before and after spellcasting
- whenever your atmosphere is tense or stale
- when moving to a new space
- after a visit from a negative or toxic guest
- whenever you want to heighten positivity around you
- after an illness
- after an argument
- anytime you just sense something is wrong.

Energetic cleansing

Energetic cleansing focuses on clearing subtle or lingering energy rather than the physical environment and so restores balance and presence to a space. It is often used to release emotional residue, mental heaviness or energetic impressions that can build up through daily life or ritual work.

This type of cleansing may involve:

- intention
- breath
- visualisation
- sound
- simple ritual actions.

For new witches especially, it is important to understand that cleansing is not a single, rigid practice. There are many approaches and none are universally correct. What matters most is awareness, intention and respect for the space you inhabit.

Cleansing is not…

- a battle against imagined forces
- a sign that you have failed spiritually
- something that must be done perfectly
- a constant, obsessive activity.

To cleanse a space, witches often work with smoke and sound. Incense or loose herbs may be burned in a heat-safe container such as a cauldron. Bound bundles of herbs commonly called smudge sticks are also widely used.

Cleansing herbs can equally be made into a room spray or simmer pot, allowing the energy of the plants to move through the home. Sound is also an effective method for cleansing. Ringing a bell or a chime is a smoke-free way to clear stagnant energy.

Sage is one of the most well-known herbs for cleansing but is considered extremely strong, often described as a kind of 'spiritual bleach'. For this reason, it is best used mindfully and only when you truly need it. It is good to follow sage with a softer, restorative herb such as a lavender or palo santo to invite warmth, balance and positivity back into space.

Common herbs for cleansing

- **White sage:** removes negative energy.
- **Lavender:** promotes relaxation and eases stress.
- **Cedar:** brings in good influences.
- **Rose:** promotes self-love.
- **Palo santo:** purifies the spirit.
- **Mugwort:** brings psychic dreams. Burn to clear stagnant energy.

EXERCISE: A CLEANSING RITUAL

You will need:

- Incense or a smudge stick of your choice

- A small heat-proof ceramic bowl or saucer
- A lighter or matches
- Optional: a small container of sand or water to extinguish safely

Instructions:

1. Begin by preparing your space. If you are using a smudge stick or incense cone, place it on the ceramic bowl or saucer before lighting. For incense sticks, simply keep the saucer nearby to catch any ash.
2. Stand tall and steady, and pause for a moment of focus. Visualise the negative energy you wish to clear from your space and imagine it dissolving into light.
3. Light your chosen smudge stick or incense. Hold the heat-proof dish underneath your smudge to catch any ash.
4. Walk slowly around your space wafting the smoke into the air. Let it drift into corners and behind doors, anywhere that feels heavy or stagnant. Move with intention, knowing that each breath of smoke is clearing and blessing the space.
5. Say the following incantation or create one of your own: '*By leaf and flame, by earth made whole, this place is cleansed in body and soul.*'
6. When finished, extinguish the smudge stick carefully by dipping the tip lightly into the sand or water making sure no embers remain. Store safely for future use. If you are burning incense, you may either allow it to burn down in a holder or gently snuff it out for reuse.
7. As the smoke clears, take a final breath and visualise your space filled with light, peace and renewal.

Magickal symbols

Symbols have always been the language of magick. Where words fall short, symbols convey deep meanings that resonate with both the conscious and subconscious mind. In witchcraft and spiritual practice, magickal symbols are more than decoration: they are tools of focus, carriers of energy and bridges between the physical and the unseen.

From the moment humanity first carved spirals on stone or painted runes onto wood, symbols have been used to connect with forces greater than ourselves. They can condense whole concepts – protection, transformation, love, divinity – into a single image. When used in ritual, these images bypass the logical mind and communicate directly with spirit, helping us channel intention and power.

The importance of magickal symbols lies in their universality. A single shape can be recognised across cultures yet hold personal resonance for the practitioner. The pentagram, for example, is one of the oldest magickal symbols. Each of the star's points represents the five elements – earth, air, fire, water and spirit – in harmony. Spirals, found in ancient carvings across Ireland and beyond, are connected to cycles of growth and evolution. The ankh of Egypt embodies eternal life, while the Celtic triquetra reflects the balance of threefold forces: body, mind and spirit or maiden, mother and crone.

In magickal practice, symbols can be drawn on tools, carved into candles, inscribed on parchment or visualised in the mind's eye. They help to concentrate energy, acting like a key that unlocks specific currents and a focus for the intention with which they are used. A protective sigil drawn on a doorway may guard a home, while a rune inscribed on a charm can attract abundance.

Magickal symbols remind us that we are part of an unbroken lineage of practitioners stretching back thousands of years. When we trace a spiral or draw a pentagram, we echo the movements of ancestors who worked with the same shapes in their rituals. They remind us that magick is both timeless and universal, and it crosses boundaries of language and culture.

At the same time, symbols are deeply personal. A simple stone carved with a rune may mean one thing in historical tradition and another to the witch who charges it with their own energy. This duality – universal and personal – is what gives symbols their enduring power.

Symbols are visual spells in themselves, carrying intention, memory and spirit. By learning and honouring magickal symbols, we strengthen both our magickal practice and our connection to the mysteries that lie beyond the veil.

EXERCISE: THE MAGICKAL KEY

Keys have long been believed to offer protection from evil and open the doors of opportunity. This door is a spiritual threshold, inviting you to step through into growth, transformation and aligned possibility. What doors of opportunity would you like to open? Write them below.

Celtic symbols and their meanings

- **Tree of life:** connection with upper and lower worlds
- **Triskele:** mind, body, spirit
- **Celtic cross:** knowledge, strength
- **Triple moon:** maiden, mother, crone
- **Spiral:** transition, growth
- **Triquetra**: natural balance and cycles of beginning, middle and end
- **Trinity knot:** creation, magick of the Goddess, spiritual union

Lunar goddess

- **Maiden:** The maiden represents youth and innocence. She symbolises the enchantment and wonder of childhood. The maiden is the beginning, the heart and soul of the cycle.
- **Mother:** The mother represents creation and fertility. She reminds us to manifest a life of conscious living and inspires us to live boldly and courageously.
- **Crone:** The crone is the wise one, the wisdom-filled elder. She offers advice and guidance.

The pentagram

The pentagram is a five-pointed star surrounded by a circle. Each point represents the five elements of earth, air, fire and water, with the upward point representing spirit. The pentagram is said to have magickal powers and is often inscribed on objects to add power to rituals. It is also a sign often used for protection from negative and harmful energies.

The pentacle

The pentacle is also a five-pointed star but enclosed within a circle, commonly used in earth-based and magickal traditions. Each point also represents the five elements, with the enclosing circle symbolising unity, wholeness and protection. It is frequently used as a protective and grounding symbol for rituals and sacred spaces. The pentacle represents balance between the material and the spiritual worlds.

Choosing your own magickal symbol

Take a quiet moment and reflect on which shapes, signs or sacred marks stir something within you. It may be a spiral (representing life's unfolding journey), a triquetra (the sacred triad of mind, body and spirit) or the tree of life (roots and branches united in balance). Trust your intuition.

Explore their stories

Research the history or mythology behind each symbol. Notice where they appear – carved into Celtic stones, woven into folklore or whispered in old prayers. See how their meanings align with your own experiences and the lessons of the elements.

Create your versions

On a page of your journal, draw three of your favourite symbols. They don't need to be perfect; what matters is that your hand shapes them. If you prefer, you can craft them from clay, paint them on cloth, carve them into wood or gather natural items to form them outdoors.

Bring them into your space

Place your symbols in your magickal space – on your altar, in a spell pouch or underneath a candle. Each time you see them, pause to breathe, remembering the qualities of growth, balance, clarity or renewal imbued within them.

By creating and honouring your own versions of these symbols, you invite the wisdom of the elements into your daily practice. They become anchors, gentle reminders that the language of magick is alive, surrounding you, waiting to be spoken.

CHAPTER 10

The art of spellcasting

Behold the art of spellcasting:
not command, but communion.

The shaping of will through word, breath and deed.

Where intention is sharpened, the unseen
is invited and the world listens.

Delve into the captivating world of mystical arts, where the possibilities are endless and magick is always in the air. With diligent practice, we can sharpen our spellcraft skills and discover a multitude of paths to explore.

However, let's not forget the importance of ethics. Our incantations should always be guided by positive intentions and never cause harm to others. Ensuring your safety should be a top priority when practising spellcasting. The art of magick forbids the casting of spells for others. Let's weave spells that radiate positivity, igniting hope and joy in ourselves and those around us. Remember, we reap what we sow, so let's sprinkle our magick with love and light.

Casting circle

Casting a circle is one of the most beautiful and grounding practices in witchcraft. A circle is more than a shape on the ground: it is a sacred container, a protective boundary between the everyday and the magickal.

Within its space, the energy you raise is held, focused and amplified, while outside influences are kept at bay. It is your temple, your sanctuary and the bridge between worlds. Cast a circle before any magickal working and close it when you are finished.

EXERCISE: HOW TO CAST CIRCLE

You will need:

- A quiet place where you feel safe
- Representations of each element, for instance feathers or incense, a candle, a bowl of water, a crystal, salt or stone.

Before you begin:

1. Choose a quiet, safe place. This may be your altar, a garden or even a small space in your room.
2. Take a few slow breaths, feeling the ground beneath your feet. Imagine roots growing down into the earth, anchoring you firmly.
3. Hold your intention close to your heart. What is the purpose of this ritual?
4. When you are ready, stand at the eastern edge of your space.

Instructions:

1. **Face east.** This is the direction of air. Imagine a soft breeze stirring. Say these words of welcome: '*Spirits of air, bring clarity, inspiration and fresh breath into this circle.*' You might wave a feather or waft incense to honour them.
2. **Face south.** Turn clockwise to the south. Here you call in fire, the spark of transformation. Light a candle, feel its warmth and say:

'Spirits of fire, ignite courage, passion and strength. Guard this circle with your flame.'

3. **Face west.** Turn to the west, the realm of water. Place a bowl of water or a shell, and say:
   'Spirits of Water, bring healing, love and flow. Wash this space clean with your sacred tides.' You may dip your fingers into the water as a sign of connection.
4. **Face north.** Finally, turn north. Touch a stone, crystal or sprinkle a little salt as you call upon earth:
   'Spirits of earth, ground me in stability and endurance. Hold this circle steady and strong.'
5. **Face the centre.** Stand quietly and open your palms. Visualise the four elements weaving together, forming a shimmering boundary around you. Then, lift your heart upwards and whisper:
   'Spirit, essence of life, unite the elements and bless this sacred space. So, it is.'
6. **The circle is now cast.** You have created a living boundary, both within and around you. Here, magick can flow freely, your intentions held safe in the embrace of the elements.
7. **Close the circle.** Thank each element in turn and release them, walking counter-clockwise to close the circle.

Casting a circle reminds us that magick is not only in the tools or the words, but in the way we choose to honour the unseen. Each time you create one, you step into alignment with earth, sky and spirit – and remember that wherever you stand can become sacred ground.

Types of spells

Incantations

Spoken words are spells in their own right. In magick, we call them incantations: focused words spoken with intention to shape energy. Just as everyday words can wound or heal, incantations ripple out into the unseen, carrying our will into action. Some practitioners also use traditional chants and words of power that have been spoken for centuries, tapping into layers of collective energy.

A favourite incantation

I vividly remember doing a banishing spell for heavy energy at a time when I was experiencing sleepless nights and the atmosphere in my home felt weighed down by a heaviness I couldn't quite shake.

I decided to try a simple incantation with herbs and candlelight. I lit a black candle and held a bundle of dried rosemary and mint. As I walked through each room, I repeated an incantation over and over: '*By flame and leaf, I clear this space, no shadow lingers, no heavy trace. With air and fire, with water and stone, this home is safe; this home is my own.*'

I spoke it aloud, steady and rhythmic, letting the words carry my will. By the time I returned to the altar and snuffed the candle, the whole space felt lighter. That night, I slept deeply for the first time in weeks. It taught me that words have power when spoken with intention, the rhythm of an incantation amplifies energy like a drumbeat for the soul.

EXERCISE: BANISHING INCANTATION SPELL

You will need:

- A black candle (for banishing)
- Rosemary and/or mint (for cleansing)
- A fire-safe dish for herbs and a lighter or matches

Instructions:

1. Light the black candle and place the herbs nearby.
2. Holding the herbs, move clockwise around your space.
3. Speak the incantation (or write your own) in a steady, repetitive tone:
   '*By flame and leaf, I clear this space, no shadow lingers, no heavy trace. With air and fire, with water and stone, this home is safe; this home is my own.*'
4. Return to the candle, sprinkle herbs into the fire-safe dish, and say:
   '*This space is clear, this space is free, by earth and sky, so may it be.*' Snuff the candle, sealing the work.

Personalising your spells

Some witches prefer to write their own spells and incantations, making their magick even more personal. Both versions are powerful. Existing spells offer rhythm and ancestral weight, while self-made incantations speak directly to the heart.

I once crafted my own chant during a time of great anxiety, whispering, '*Peace within, peace without, ease my spirit, calm my doubt.*' Repeated three times, the words calmed my racing thoughts and helped me reclaim my balance.

The paper lantern

A few winters ago, I was feeling stuck. Work felt stagnant and I couldn't see what direction to take next. I didn't want a dramatic upheaval, just a gentle nudge from the universe. I needed a sign that I was on the right path.

One evening, I sat at my kitchen table with a candle, a pen and a sheet of paper. I wrote down a single word that kept resurfacing in my journalling: 'growth'. Around it, I sketched vines curling into leaves and tiny buds. As I drew, I spoke softly to myself, almost like a mantra: '*With every line, I plant a seed. What's meant for me will find its way.*'

When the ink dried, I folded the paper into a small packet and placed it in a glass jar. I set the jar beside the candle and let the flame burn down as I visualised doors opening and opportunities arriving. I kept the folded paper and tucked it inside my journal, a quiet reminder to stay open to change.

Within a month, an unexpected opportunity came my way through an old acquaintance. It wasn't what I had imagined, but it led me into a new circle of people and a career shift that felt so much more aligned. Looking back, I can see how writing that single word and charging it with intention acted as a beacon, drawing in the growth I'd asked for.

Spell tokens

Magick thrives when spirit meets matter. Through ritual and spellwork, objects become charged with power. A poppet, pouch or token holds intention and can be carried on the person, laid upon an altar or safely disposed of in order to promote a spell. The token can be a pouch of herbs for protection, an amulet worn against negativity or even a small stone carved with a spiral.

The abundance spell bag

One evening I decided to craft my first abundance spell bag. It was winter and I felt a little depleted: my energy, my wallet and my creativity all seemed to be running thin. I wanted to remind myself that prosperity isn't just about money, but about living in a flow of opportunity, nourishment and satisfaction.

I gathered a small square of green cloth and set it on my altar. I had picked and dried marigold petals earlier in the year; their bright orange and gold colour seemed to radiate sunlight even in the dim light of my room. I placed them in the centre of the cloth. Next came a small piece of citrine, warm and honey-coloured in my palm. To me, it symbolised the spark of optimism and the magnetism of prosperity. I tucked it carefully into the cloth. I sprinkled in a pinch of green salt (salt that I coloured with green food dye) to ground the spell and remind me that true wealth is rooted in the earth's abundance.

I then wrote a few words on a slip of paper: '*May abundance flow into my life with ease, bringing security and joy.*' I folded the note and placed it with the other items, feeling as though I had planted a seed. I then folded the cloth so it created a tight bundle and tied the spell bag closed with string.

When it was complete, I let each element bless it: holding it over a candle's flame, passing it through incense smoke, above the water bowl and pressing it to stone. I kept it on my altar, occasionally refreshing it with new herbs or setting it in sunlight to charge the citrine.

In the weeks that followed, I noticed little shifts. More than anything, the spell bag reminded me that abundance is an energy I can invite in – and that the simple act of creating something with love and intention can open the door to receiving.

Spell jars

Spell jars are simply a collection of magickal items gathered and kept together in a small container, charged with ritual and intention, which work together to manifest a specific outcome. Spell jars are popular vessels for luck, prosperity, love or protection magick, but you can customise them any way you like with any magickal ingredients, elements or tools that resonate with your intention.

EXERCISE: CREATE YOUR OWN SPELL JAR

To create your own spell jar, simply place items that resonate with your intention together in a jar. Then write your intention on a piece of paper, fold it and bury it underneath the contents. Keep the spell jar on your altar or within your home to attract what you desire.

You will need:

- Pen and paper for your written affirmation
- A small, clean jar
- Magickal ingredients that correspond to your intention

Here are some suggested intentions and corresponding ingredients:

- **Self-love:** red or pink salt, a rose quartz crystal, rose petals, rose oil, lavender oil
- **Money and abundance:** green salt, a citrine crystal, a bay leaf, calendula petals, peppermint, a coin
- **Protection:** black salt, a black onyx crystal, rosemary oil

Instructions:

1. Place the salt, herbs and petals into the jar.
2. Bury the crystal underneath the herbs, petals and salt.
3. Write your intention on a piece of paper.
4. Fold and bury in the salt and petals with the crystal.
5. Place the spell jar on your altar or anywhere around your home and let it do its work.

What do you wish for? Write your wishes in the spell jars.

Tools for spell crafting

Magickal tools are more than objects; they are companions on the journey of spirit. A wand is not simply wood, nor is a chalice just a cup: they are vessels through which energy flows between the realms of the seen and unseen. Tools give form to our intention, making what is whispered within the heart into something we can witness, hold and direct.

We use tools not because magick requires them, but because we do. They focus the mind, awaken the senses and root our rituals in the physical world. When you strike a match to light a candle, when you scatter herbs into a bowl or trace a circle with a blade, you are calling your will into action.

Ultimately, it is not the tools that hold the magick, but the witch who uses them. Power does not reside in the wand or chalice, but in a witch's will, awareness and intention. Tools do not create magick, they channel it. They act as an extension of a witch's energy, focusing and giving shape to what already exists within.

Every tool is symbolic: the chalice of water, the blade of air, the wand of fire, the pentacle of earth. But tools can also be humble. They can be stones from the roadside, shells from the shore, a key, a feather, a piece of string. What matters is not grandeur but meaning. In practical magick, tools are reminders that the divine is woven into everything, waiting to be awakened by our touch.

Below are some common tools.

Angel numbers

Angel numbers are repeating number patterns – such as 111, 222 or 555 – that many believe carry guidance from the spiritual realm. They appear in everyday places: on clocks, receipts, car plates or phone numbers, catching your eye just when you need reassurance.

The idea of angel numbers is rooted in numerology, an ancient system that views numbers as carriers of vibrational energy. Modern spiritual practice has woven this into the belief that angels and guides (or the universe) use numbers as a subtle language to reach us and remind us that we never truly walk alone.

- 111: Trust your intuition.
- 222: You are where you need to be at this time.
- 333: Encouragement from your guides.
- 444: You are being protected by your spiritual guides.
- 555: A change is on the horizon.
- 666: Embrace your spiritual awareness.
- 777: Luck is all around you.
- 888: Everything is falling into place.
- 999: Let go of what no longer serves you.

Brooms and besoms

Brooms were traditionally used to cast circles for spells. Mini brooms, also known as besoms, are often carried as amulets and placed inside the home or above a door for protection. They are a symbol of power and intention.

The broomstick is also a symbol of inner flight. The witch flying on a broomstick is not about escape, but speaks to the inner knowing that the witch does not wait for permission to move beyond limitation. The broom becomes a symbol of transformation reminding us that power is not just found in grand artefacts, but also in the ability to shift consciousness, to rise above and to journey between the seen and unseen.

Cauldrons

The cauldron is one of the oldest symbols of witchcraft, representing transformation, creation, rebirth and the element of earth. In Celtic mythology, it is linked to Cerridwen, whose cauldron was a vessel of wisdom, inspiration and magickal knowledge. It is also associated with Wiccan rituals and beliefs. The cauldron is often seen as the womb of the Goddess – dark, fertile and full of mystery – where raw ingredients are stirred and transformed, just as experiences shape the soul.

In ritual, the cauldron is a symbol of potential and renewal, echoing the mythic promise that from the cauldron, new life and wisdom are continually born. In practical use, the cauldron is used as a heat-safe vessel for burning herbs and resins or affirmation papers lit on fire. Disc charcoal is the best fuel for a cauldron, but be sure to use this in a well-ventilated area.

What's brewing in the magickal cauldron of yours? Write it below.

Colours and candles

Candles embody transformation and the element of fire. Wax becomes flame, symbolising the desire made to manifest. The flame represents spirit, focus and illumination.

In candle magick, the colour of the candle is often chosen to reflect the intention of the work, honour deities, mark elements or release energy. The candle's colour becomes a focal point, helping to anchor the intention throughout the ritual. Candle colours that align with the purpose of a spell will amplify it.

White

White is the most versatile candle colour and may be used in place of any other colour. White is associated with cleansing, peace and spiritual connection. White candles are commonly used for blessing rituals, ancestral work and when simplicity or neutrality is required.

Black

Black candles are used for protection, banishing, uncrossing and the absorption of negative energies. Contrary to popular belief, black is not harmful. It is grounding and containing. It is particularly effective in boundary-setting work and rituals of release.

Red

Red is the colour of vitality, strength, courage and passion. It is often used in spells relating to desire, motivation and confidence. Red also carries protective qualities and offers a boost of strength and resolve.

Pink

Pink relates to gentler emotional energy such as self-love, compassion, friendship and emotion. It is commonly used in heart-centred work for softness and care, rather than intensity.

Green

Green is associated with growth, abundance, prosperity and connection to the natural world. It is frequently used in money work, healing rituals and spells focused on sustainable progress.

Blue

Blue supports calm communication, emotional balance and inner peace. It is suited to rituals involving healing, sleep, anxiety reduction and finding your voice.

Yellow

Yellow corresponds with confidence, creativity and clarity. It is often used for study, decision making and work that requires focus or mental sharpness.

Purple

Purple is linked with intuition, spiritual insight, wisdom and higher consciousness. It is commonly used in meditation, divination and dreamwork, as well as rituals that seek deep understanding.

Orange

Orange blends creativity and action. It is associated with opportunity, motivation and success, particularly for career or other goals.

Brown

Brown is grounding and practical. It is used for stability, property and home matters. It is also excellent for situations that require common sense, security and a steady foundation.

Gold and silver

Gold represents success, confidence, solar energy and achievement, while silver represents intuition, lunar energy, reflection and emotional wisdom. These colours are often used to honour cycles, energetic balance and personal power.

And a practical note

Candle colour enhances intention but does not override it. Focused attention and a clearly-held purpose are far more important than the perfect correspondence. When in doubt, choose the colour that feels most aligned to you or use white as a universal substitute.

Colours beyond candle magick

Colour correspondence is not just for candle magick. Colours can also be incorporated subtly through clothing, jewellery or personal items. Wearing a particular colour, or carrying a crystal in a matching tone can act as a quiet reinforcement of intention throughout the day. For example, green clothing or jewellery may be chosen to support abundance or growth, while black may be worn for grounding or protection. These small choices allow ritual intention to extend beyond formal practice and into everyday life.

The same principles apply to crystals, where colour can influence how a stone is selected or used. While green crystals are commonly associated with abundance, blue crystals are linked with expression and speaking one's truth. In this way, colour can be seen as just as meaningful as the stone itself, guiding intuitive choices and supporting consistency across ritual work.

Dressing candles

Witches also 'dress candles' by applying sacred oils and herbs to the candle to aid a spell's intention.

- To bring something to you, rub oil from the top of the candle downwards, then bottom to the middle.
- To release or banish something, apply oil from the middle to the ends.

We do not rub back and forth because intention requires steadiness. Dab the remaining oil onto your third eye and breastbone, and state your intent.

Essential oils

Essential oils are concentrated plant essences, distilled from leaves, flowers, woods and resins. In magick, they are used to shift energy, awaken the senses and amplify intention. Their scents move quickly through the body and spirit, making them powerful allies for ritual and spellwork. They are a great option for witches without easy access to fresh or dried herbs.

You might place a few drops in an oil burner or diffuser to fill your space with the energy you wish to cultivate. Oils can also be blended into anointing mixtures for candles, crystals or ritual tools, or added to carrier oils to anoint your own body before spellcasting. A few drops in a bath create a sacred cleansing ritual, washing away negativity and restoring balance.

Each oil carries its own correspondence:

- Lavender for peace and healing
- Chamomile for rest
- Rosemary for clarity and protection
- Frankincense for spiritual connection
- Peppermint for focus and energy

Blending oils allows you to create personalised potions. For example, lavender and chamomile for calm, or rosemary and frankincense for psychic protection.

Disclaimer: Never ingest essential oils. If applying to the skin, blend one drop with a carrier oil such as almond, jojoba or olive. Essential oils may not be safe for children or pets. Remember, a little goes a long way – trust their concentrated power.

Familiars

A familiar is a spiritual ally – often appearing as an animal – who supports and protects a witch in magickal work. They are reminders that we are not alone in our craft and that we have allies in both the seen and unseen worlds. In folklore, familiars were seen as witches' companions who offered wisdom and power.

Unlike pets, familiars are believed to share a deeper energetic bond, acting as guides, guardians and messengers between worlds. And unlike spirit animals, familiars are external spirit companions who work *with you* in magick, whereas spirit animals reflect inner qualities, guidance or life lessons.

Familiars can take many forms. Cats are the most famous, symbolising mystery, independence and protection. Dogs embody loyalty and guardianship. Birds bring messages and vision, while toads and snakes represent transformation and healing. The qualities of a familiar will depend on its nature: a cat may sharpen intuition, while a raven encourages insight into hidden truths.

Incense

Incense refers to a substance that produces a pleasant aroma when burned. The use of incense has been around for thousands of years and is a significant part of many cultures and religions around the world. Associated with the element of air, there are various types of incense, each with its unique scent and properties.

- Nag Champa has a musky, earthy scent and is made from a blend of sandalwood and other natural ingredients. It is popularly used in meditation and yoga practices.
- Frankincense has a sweet and woody scent that is often used in religious ceremonies. Its use dates back centuries and it is believed to have healing properties.
- Lavender has a calming and soothing scent, often used to promote relaxation and sleep.
- Jasmine has a sweet and floral scent. It is believed to have aphrodisiac properties.

- Patchouli has a strong, earthy scent and is believed to promote grounding and stability.
- Sandalwood has a warm and comforting scent, believed to promote relaxation and reduce anxiety and stress. Sandalwood incense is often used in aromatherapy and meditation practices.

CHAPTER 11

Magick for wellbeing

People rarely come to magick by accident. Most arrive at its threshold seeking comfort, guidance or a spark of hope when life feels heavy. They will come with questions, longings and unseen wounds. Magick offers a lantern in the dark.

Practical magick is not an escape from reality, but a way to work with it: gently shifting energy, bringing clarity where there is confusion, courage where there is fear and peace where there is unrest.

Magick for wellbeing is about creating harmony between the inner and outer worlds. A simple candle flame can steady the mind; a whispered incantation can quiet the heart. Herbs, oils, crystals and charms are tools that remind us of our power to heal, transform and release. Whether it's a ritual bath to wash away stress, a pouch of herbs under the pillow for restful sleep or a rune cast for insight, magick offers practical ways to nurture body, mind and spirit.

Here lies the beauty of this path: magick meets you where you are. If you are anxious, there is protection and grounding. If you are weary, there is renewal and strength. If you are lost, there is guidance and vision. Each tool and each spell becomes a companion, helping you align with the rhythms of nature and the wisdom within yourself.

What follows is a list of the most common areas where practical magick can offer support: love, protection, healing, abundance, clarity – and more. Let these be starting points, guiding lights on your own journey. Take what resonates, shape it with your own intention and know that magick for wellbeing is always an act of self-care. At its core, it is a reminder that you are worthy of peace, joy and wholeness.

Abundance, wealth and success

Some of the most common questions I receive in my work are about abundance. People often approach magick hoping to attract wealth, success and opportunity into their lives.

It makes sense – money provides security, stability and freedom of choice. Success, in its many forms, provides a sense of purpose and achievement. Abundance allows us to not only meet our needs, but to dream bigger, create and share.

Yet I've noticed that behind the desire for money or success, there is often a deeper longing.

Does having all the abundance the universe can give automatically make people happy and content? People often assume yes. But true abundance is more than coins or possessions, it is a state of flow where resources, opportunities and joy circulate freely in life.

I remember a time when I desperately wished for financial relief. I performed a small abundance spell, placing a coin under a green candle and repeating, '*Prosperity flows, my needs are met.*'

Within days, an unexpected payment came through. The spell didn't just bring money, it restored my sense of hope. And this is the true essence of abundance magick: it does not bring wealth for wealth's sake; it brings the freedom, peace and possibility that abundance awakens.

Magickal correspondences for abundance, wealth and success

Colours

- **Gold:** traditionally associated with abundance, prosperity and sustained success. It carries solar energy, symbolising confidence and the attraction of opportunity.
- **Green:** the colour of growth, renewal and steady prosperity. It symbolises abundance that is organically rooted in patience, rather than sudden gain.

Crystals

- **Citrine:** strongly associated with abundance, confidence and positive momentum. It is believed to attract success and abundance.
- **Tiger's eye:** associated with grounded abundance and personal power, and it supports wise decision making around money and resources.

Essential oils and incense

- **Cinnamon:** traditionally linked to money flow, abundance and prosperity. Use sparingly: it is potent and stimulating.
- **Frankincense:** elevates abundance intentions, often used in prosperity work.
- **Myrrh:** promotes slow, stable wealth growth and protection of long-term resources.

- **Patchouli:** excellent for promoting sustained prosperity, frequently used as a base oil in money-drawing blends.

Herb, plant and tree allies

Throughout history, witches and wise folk have turned to plants as allies in attracting prosperity, removing obstacles and drawing good fortune. Each herb, plant and tree carries its own vibration and gift, ready to be woven into charms, floor washes or everyday rituals.

- **Angelica root:** powerful protector and attractor of blessings. Place angelica root in your home or keep it on your altar to draw abundance and safeguard the prosperity that enters your space.
- **Basil:** known as the witch's herb of wealth. Add basil to your mop bucket when cleansing floors to invite prosperity and good fortune to flow through the heart of your home.
- **Calamus root:** used in money-drawing spells, strengthens intention and helps attract steady financial gain. Carry a piece with you or add it to prosperity sachets to call wealth closer.
- **Ginkgo leaves:** resilience and longevity. Gingko leaves are especially powerful in money magick, ensuring wealth that lasts and opportunities that grow.
- **Lemongrass:** clears away blockages and stagnant energy. Bright and refreshing, it removes obstacles to prosperity, brings luck and opens doors that once seemed closed.

- **Woodruff:** traditional charm of victory and success. Place a pinch in your left shoe when you need luck on your side, ensuring that your steps lead to triumph.

Spirit animals

These animals remind us that abundance isn't just about money. It's about growth, flow and living in harmony with life's cycles.

The hare is a sacred and mystical symbol and has traditionally been associated with the Goddess Brigid. To the Celts, the hare was linked with the full moon, night and the supernatural. The hare embodies gentleness, cleverness and romance, and is said the hare is able to jump between the spiritual realms.

- **Hare:** luck, prosperity and intuition.
- **Deer:** grace, gentleness, and opportunities flowing naturally; abundance through harmony with nature.
- **Butterfly:** transformation, renewal and flourishing; abundance that comes from growth.
- **Peacock:** beauty, pride and richness of spirit; abundance as a celebration of life's gifts.

EXERCISE: A SPELL FOR ABUNDANCE, MONEY-DRAWING, PROSPERITY AND LUCK

This spell draws on the energy of crystals, herbs and flame to attract prosperity and abundance. For best results, cast this spell on a Wednesday, which is ruled by Mercury, the planet of communication and flow.

You will need:

- 1 citrine crystal
- Green salt
- 1 bay leaf
- A sprig of peppermint (or dried leaves)
- 1 coin
- 1 green candle
- Cinnamon oil
- Calendula flowers
- A lighter or matches and a heat-proof dish
- A small piece of paper with a written affirmation (e.g. '*Abundance flows easily into my life.*')

Instructions:

1. Place the citrine crystal at the centre of your working surface.
2. Sprinkle green salt over it, forming a small mound.
3. Add the bay leaf, peppermint and coin.
4. Tuck your written affirmation beneath the crystal or salt.
5. Anoint the green candle with cinnamon oil. Draw the oil from top to middle, then bottom to middle, to pull energy into the centre.
6. Place the candle in a heat-proof dish. Surround its base with calendula flowers, symbols of success and prosperity.

7. Light the candle.
8. Focus on your intention. See abundance flowing towards you like sunlight, steady and golden. Say aloud your affirmation or create your own words of power.
9. Allow the candle to burn down safely, or snuff it and relight each Wednesday until your goal feels fulfilled. Keep the coin or citrine with you as a charm of ongoing prosperity.

Peace and calm

In a world that rarely slows down, finding calm can feel like a luxury. We are surrounded by noise: not only the hum of traffic and technology, but a constant, never-ending stream of thoughts, worries and demands. This is why magick for calm and peace is so vital. It permits us to soften, rest and remember that serenity is something that we can always cultivate within ourselves, here and now.

I remember a time when my mind felt like a storm. Between work, family, commitments and the weight of unspoken worries, my thoughts spun in endless circles. One evening, I gathered a small blue candle, a bowl of water and a sprig of lavender from my garden. I lit the candle and watched its steady flame. Then I dipped my fingers into the cool water, anointing my temples as I whispered '*Peace within, peace around. Let calm within my soul be found.*'

Something shifted in that moment. The weight in my chest eased. My breath steadied and slowed as I watched the flicker of the candle and the scent of lavender wrapped around me like a soft blanket. It wasn't that all my problems vanished – that is not something magick can do – but the chaos inside me grew quieter and I felt held by the simple magick of that small ritual.

Peace spells remind us that calmness is not weakness; it is a state of strength.

Magickal correspondences for peace and calm

Colours

- **Green and blue:** emotional balance, calms and soothes energy, creates a peaceful atmosphere.

Crystals

- **Unakite:** a gentle stone for emotional calm, helping to harmonise the heart and mind.
- **Amethyst:** known as the natural tranquiliser. It dispels anger, rage and anxiety, and brings serenity.
- **Clear quartz:** the master healer stone. It releases, regulates and balances energy to restore peace.
- **Tiger's eye:** energises the emotions, alleviates depression and balances yin and yang to lift the mood.

Essential oils and incense

- **Nag Champa:** sacred incense for meditation and yoga that encourages calm and centres focus.
- **Sandalwood:** calms the mind, reduces stress and anxiety, and deepens relaxation.
- **Rose:** promotes relaxation, self-love and restful sleep.

- **Vanilla:** inspires a sense of wellbeing and comfort, warming the spirit.

Herb, plant and tree allies

- **Chamomile:** comforts the spirit, eases tension, brings peace to the heart and calms restless moods. Sprinkle in bathwater to wash away quarrels and soothe the soul.
- **Hazel:** awakens quiet wisdom and clear thought. It brings mental stillness, helping the mind rest and focus. Drop its nut in running water to divine truth and hidden knowledge.
- **Lavender:** softens anxiety and encourages deep relaxation. It is a classic companion for sleep, serenity and gentle protection. Tuck a sprig underneath your pillow to keep away bad dreams and restless spirits.
- **Meadowsweet:** lifts heavy energies and restores harmony in the home. It inspires a lightness of being and a peaceful atmosphere. Scatter on the floor to sweeten the home and invite peace.
- **Oak:** deep stability and inner strength. Its steady presence restores balance and grounds scattered energy. Carry a piece for strength in times of fear or dispute.
- **Willow:** brings release from emotional burdens, allowing grief and worry to flow away. Sit beneath her boughs to weep your sorrows and rise lighter of heart.

Spirit animals

- **Deer:** gentle and graceful, the deer teaches us to move softly through life, finding peace in stillness and compassion in the heart. Its presence reminds us to approach challenges with patience and kindness.
- **Dolphin:** symbol of harmony and play, the dolphin carries the medicine of joy and emotional balance. It encourages us to breathe deeply, release stress and flow with the rhythms of life.
- **Butterfly:** light and delicate, the butterfly brings calm through transformation. It reminds us that change does not need to be turbulent, but can be graceful, natural and full of renewal.
- **Turtle:** slow and steady, the turtle embodies grounded peace. Its spirit encourages patience, resilience and the wisdom of taking life one step at a time.

EXERCISE: A SPELL TO RELIEVE ANXIETY

This spell is offered as a quiet support in moments of anxiety, helping to soften the breath and steady the moment.

You will need:

- A cleansing herb
- Pen and paper
- Salt
- A lighter or matches and a heat-proof dish

Instructions:

1. Write your worries and fears onto the paper.
2. Smudge with palo santo or white sage.
3. Burn the paper immediately or circle the paper with salt and leave for 24 hours, then burn.

What are the sources of your anxieties? Write them down and imagine you will be sealing them in the box below.

EXERCISE: A GROUNDING EXERCISE TO BRING ABOUT CALM IN TIMES OF ANXIETY

This grounding exercise is offered as a quiet support in moments of anxiety. It will help to soften the breath and steady the moment. It is kept deliberately short, recognising that when the mind feels restless or overwhelmed, simplicity is best.

- When anxiety feels present, take a few slow breaths and bring your attention to the body.
- Notice where you feel tension, and with each exhale, allow this tension to soften slightly.
- Afterwards write a short note in your journal about what you noticed, without analysing or judging.

Grounding and stability

In a world that moves too quickly, grounding and stability are not luxuries. They are essentials. To be grounded is to feel anchored, rooted and safe, even when life feels uncertain or overwhelming. Stability gives us a sense of belonging and a steady foundation from which growth becomes possible. Without it, we can feel scattered, restless or swept up in worries that are not truly ours to carry.

I remember a morning when everything felt too heavy. My mind was rushing, my body was tense. I slipped outside barefoot and stood on the damp grass. The earth was cool and soft, yet unyielding beneath me.

As I slowly breathed, I felt my thoughts quieten. My heartbeat steadied and I realised that the ground had been holding me all along. In that moment, I knew I didn't have to do everything alone. I could lean into the strength of the earth itself.

This is why creating practices for grounding and stability matter. Whether you keep a stone on your altar, sprinkle protective herbs by your doorway or simply walk among trees, these acts signal to your spirit: '*You are safe. You are rooted. You belong.*'

From that rootedness, magick flows with ease.

Correspondences for grounding and stability

Colours

- **Brown:** a reminder of your connection to the earth. Burn brown candles when you need stability, balance or to feel firmly rooted.
- **Green:** a reminder of the cycles of nature and the abundance of the living world.
- **Black:** protective and steadying. Burn black candles to remove negativity, anchor your energy and shield you from interference.
- **Blue:** emotionally grounding. Burn blue candles to help to steady racing thoughts and soothe anxiety, restoring inner stability.

Crystals

- **Hematite:** anchors you deeply in presence.
- **Red jasper:** grounding.
- **Black obsidian:** grounding and protecting.

Essential oils and incense

- **Cedarwood:** anchors your energy and connects you to the steady strength of the earth.
- **Patchouli:** brings balance, grounding and a sense of being rooted in your body.
- **Frankincense:** encourages spiritual grounding while easing worry and overthinking.

Herb, plant and tree allies

- **Hawthorn:** grounds the heart and provides protection and emotional stability. It was traditionally used to weave May Day garlands to bless and safeguard the threshold of the seasons.
- **Mugwort:** a plant of dreamwork and psychic grounding. It guides visions with clarity. Place a sprig beneath your pillow to invite true and prophetic dreams.
- **Sage:** purifies energy, clears away negativity and centres the spirit. Waft smoke through rooms to guard against unseen harm.
- **Meadowsweet:** encourages peace, calm and emotional stability in the home. It was traditionally scattered on floors to sweeten gatherings and soothe quarrels.

- **Rosemary:** protective and purifying, strengthening focus and anchoring the mind. 'Where rosemary grows, the mistress rules,' the old saying goes.

Sometimes called the Lady of the Woods, Birch (Betula pendula) is a tree of renewal and resilience. Its pale bark and flexible branches remind us that true stability is not rigid but adaptable. In magick, birch is used for grounding, cleansing and restoring balance after times of upheaval.

Spirit animals

- **Bear:** embodies strength, protection and a deep connection to the earth's cycles.
- **Stag/deer:** connects us to the earth and the forest, guiding us with quiet resilience.
- **Wolf:** grounds us in instinct, community and trust in the natural order.

EXERCISE: A GROUNDING HERBAL POUCH

You will need:

- Dried herbs such as rosemary or lavender
- A small fabric pouch or square of cloth
- A grounding crystal such as hematite
- Pen and paper

Instructions:

1. Add a pinch of each dried herb to the pouch. Then place the hematite crystal in the middle of the herbs.
2. On a slip of paper, write an intention, such as '*I am grounded and safe*.' Or you can use any grounding intention that comes to mind. Sometimes something as simple as '*I am okay*' is enough to ground you back into the present moment.
3. Seal the pouch or securely tie the piece of cloth closed.
4. Take a deep breath and close the ritual.

Uses:

Keep the pouch in your bag or on your desk – or wherever you most need grounding.

- When you next feel scattered or overwhelmed, hold the pouch in one hand and take three slow breaths.
- Bring your attention to the pouch's scent and texture and its weight in your palm.
- Name silently or out loud three things you can feel in this moment. For example, the pouch in your hand, your feet on the floor and the air on your skin.
- Say a simple incantation such as '*I return to the present*,' then continue with your day.

Healing and wellness

So often people turn to magick when their hearts feel heavy or their bodies weary. Life is full of moments that bruise the spirit as well as the body. Healing and wellness are among our deepest needs.

We seek relief from pain, balance in our emotions and the strength to keep moving forward. Magick doesn't replace medicine, but it can work alongside it – supporting our healing journey, soothing the soul and restoring a sense of wholeness when we feel fractured.

I remember a time when I felt drained, both physically and emotionally, carrying the weight of stress on my shoulders. I created a small healing ritual. I lit a lavender-scented candle, held an amethyst in my hand, and wrote the words '*I welcome peace and renewal*' on a slip of paper. As I breathed in the calming scent of lavender, I felt myself soften, as if I had given my spirit permission to rest. It didn't solve everything at once, but it gave me the strength to keep going, one step at a time.

Healing and wellness are not luxuries. They are foundational needs. Magick helps us remember that we are worthy of care, and that tending to ourselves is itself a sacred act.

Magickal correspondences for healing and wellness

Colours

- **Green:** healing and renewal, linked to balance, vitality and emotional harmony.
- **Blue:** brings calm, peace and rest; perfect for easing stress, anxiety or sleep troubles.
- **White:** pure healing light that cleanses, restores and amplifies all positive intentions.
- **Pink:** nurtures self-love, compassion and emotional healing of the heart.

Crystals

- **Citrine:** a stone of joy and vitality, uplifting the spirit and encouraging confidence. It brings warmth, positivity and abundance into daily life.
- **Black obsidian:** offers protection, absorbs negativity and grounds the soul. Helps release emotional blockages preventing true healing.
- **Clear quartz:** known as the master healer, amplifies energy and intentions, and restores balance, clarity and overall wellbeing.

Essential oils and incense

- **Cinnamon:** warming and energising. It stimulates vitality and restores motivation. Used in folk magick for health, protection and strength.
- **Copal:** a sacred resin burned to cleanse spaces and uplift the spirit. Invites light, harmony and spiritual renewal.
- **Frankincense:** calming and purifying. It clears stagnant energy, supports deep breath and was traditionally used for healing.
- **Sandalwood:** grounding and sacred. It eases tension, enhances meditation and strengthens inner peace and spiritual alignment.

Herb, plant and tree allies

- **Spruce needles:** carrier of the fresh, resinous power of the forest. Clears stagnant energy and strengthens the body's vitality. Traditionally burned or infused to restore balance and support resilience, or hung above the doorway to guard the home and keep sickness out.

- **Angelica root:** a protective and purifying root, once carried to ward off illness. Supports strength, eases sickness and uplifts the spirit during times of recovery. Carried as a charm against plague and evil spirits and said to bloom on St Michael's Day.
- **Damiana:** fragrant ally for the heart and mind, damiana is known to lift the mood, elevate low spirits and spark joy. Folklore holds it as a plant of love and light-heartedness, often brewed as a love potion and joy-herb to kindle the heart and gladden the spirit.
- **Hazel:** brings wisdom, clarity and restores psychic balance. Hazelnuts were once believed to hold sacred knowledge and healing powers, and water from a hazel well was said to cure many ills. Hazel twigs were woven into protective charms, carried to ward off evil spirits and misfortune.

Spirit animals

- **Butterfly:** a symbol of transformation and renewal, guiding you through cycles of healing and change.
- **Snake:** represents rebirth, shedding the old to allow the body and spirit to regenerate.
- **Deer:** brings gentle healing energy, soothing emotional wounds with compassion and grace.
- **Owl:** offers wisdom and insight, helping you see the root of what needs to heal.

EXERCISE: A SIMPLE HEALING SPELL

This spell is designed to soothe the heart, calm the mind and invite the body back into balance. You don't need anything elaborate, just your intention, a candle and a few simple allies from nature.

You will need:

- 1 blue or white candle (for peace and healing) and a lighter or matches
- 1 small piece of amethyst or clear quartz, if you have it
- Pen and paper
- A few drops of rose oil or lavender oil

Instructions:

1. Begin by finding a quiet space. Light your candle and watch the flame grow steady.
2. Hold the crystal in your hand and take a few deep breaths, imagining roots stretching down into the earth, grounding and steadying you.
3. On the paper, write a simple intention such as:
   '*I welcome healing, peace and renewal into every part of me.*'
4. Fold the paper three times, anoint it with a drop of oil and place it beneath the candle.
5. Gently whisper:
   '*Light of healing, flame so true. Restore my spirit, my body anew. With every breath, my strength I claim. Peace and balance in my name.*'

6. Let the candle burn safely for a while, then extinguish it. Carry the crystal and your written intention with you as a reminder that healing is already unfolding.

EXERCISE: A SIMPLE HEALING RITUAL

Healing rituals are about creating a sacred moment to rest, release, and restore your spirit. This ritual is gentle and supportive, helping you invite peace and balance back into your life.

You will need:

- A bowl of warm water with a pinch of salt (for cleansing)
- 1 blue or white candle (for calm and healing)
- A small amethyst or clear quartz crystal, if you have it
- A few drops of lavender or rose oil (for soothing energy)

Instructions:

1. Find a quiet space where you won't be disturbed. Place the bowl of salted water in front of you, set the candle beside it, and rest the crystal nearby.
2. Light the candle, focusing on the steady flame.
3. Add a drop or two of oil into the water, swirling it gently with your finger.
4. Dip your fingertips into the water, then touch it lightly to your forehead, heart and hands, saying:
   '*By water's grace and fire's light, I call in healing, calm and might. Release the pain. Let peace remain. I am whole and well again.*'

5. Sit quietly for a few minutes, breathing deeply, letting the flame and scented water wash away tension. When ready, extinguish the candle. Keep the crystal as your healing ally.

What came up for you in this healing ritual? Name your thoughts. Write them in the wreaths.

Write a letter to yourself. Tell yourself how well you're doing despite any obstacles you may have faced.

Love, fertility and attraction

Love is one of the most powerful forces, an energy that shapes our lives as much as the moon shapes the tides. When people come to me with questions about magick, love and attraction are often at the very top of the list. Some long to call a partner into their life, others wish to deepen an existing bond and many simply seek to fall in love with themselves again. Fertility, too, is a theme that arises frequently, not only in the sense of creating new life, but also in nurturing creativity, new projects or personal growth.

At its heart, love magick is rarely about bending someone else's will. Work that seeks to override another person's autonomy crosses into baneful territory and often carries unintended consequences. Spells rooted in control or manipulation may not bring the connection desired and instead create imbalance, entanglement and resentment. For this reason, spells for love should be focused on self-worth, clarity, attraction and alignment – trusting that genuine connection arises through consent, choice and mutual resonance, rather than force.

Once, after I really neglected my own self-care, I crafted a small charm bag. I filled it with rose petals, a piece of rose quartz and a handwritten affirmation: '*I am open to nourishing myself.*' Carrying it was a daily reminder that love begins within and that self-acceptance attracts relationships of equal care. The spell shifted how I treated myself and in time made self-care a daily practice.

Magickal correspondences for love, fertility and attraction

Colours

- **Pink:** nurturing love, emotional healing and gentle self-compassion.
- **Red:** vitality, passion and life-force energy.
- **White:** purity, balance and overall wellbeing.

Crystals

- **Rose quartz:** the stone of unconditional love, soothing the heart and restoring emotional balance.
- **Garnet:** energises the body and spirit, sparking vitality while grounding strength.
- **Ruby:** a gem of passion and wellness, inspiring courage, warmth and life-affirming energy.

Essential oils and incense

- **Lavender:** calms the mind and body, easing stress and tension.
- **Patchouli:** grounding, earthy and restorative, reconnecting you to stability.
- **Rose:** opens the heart, bringing comfort, self-love and emotional healing.

- **Ylang-ylang:** sweetly soothing, balancing emotions and softening anxious thoughts.

Herb, plant and tree allies

- **Creeping cinquefoil:** encourages romantic opportunities and strengthens bonds, especially in new or uncertain relationships. Place beneath the pillow to dream of a future lover's face.
- **Lovage:** long been linked with passion and attraction. It stirs desire and invites affection. Young women once tucked lovage into their clothes to make themselves irresistible.
- **Meadowsweet:** brings harmony, joy and peace to relationships, easing tension and softening hearts. It was traditionally used in bridal garlands and thought to bless unions with harmony and sweetness.
- **Oak:** also known as 'potent wood'. Associated with strength, fertility, grounding and longevity in love. Carrying an acorn was said to attract lasting love and steady marriage.

The apple (Malus domestica) is linked with beauty, desire and fertility, making it a powerful symbol of love and romance magick. In Celtic lore, apples were considered a gateway to the otherworld, where eternal love and abundance flourish. Folk tradition held that cutting an apple crosswise reveals the five-pointed star within, a symbol of magick and attraction.

Spirit animals

- **Cat:** symbol of sensuality, mystery and independence; teaches us self-love and magnetism.
- **Swan:** represents beauty, grace and the deep soul-bond of true love.
- **Butterfly:** inspires transformation in matters of the heart, opening space for new love.
- **Frog:** linked with fertility, emotional renewal and refreshed energy.

EXERCISE: A SPELL TO OPEN YOUR HEART TO LOVE AND SELF-LOVE

This spell is designed to open your heart to love, whether you are calling a new partner, deepening an existing bond or nurturing self-love.

You will need:

- 1 pink candle (for love and tenderness)
- Pen and paper
- 1 rose quartz crystal (for love and compassion)
- A few rose petals (for romance and sweetness)
- A heat-proof surface or saucer and a lighter or matches
- A pinch of pink salt (for purification and gentle protection)
- 1–2 drops of rose oil (to open the heart)
- 1–2 drops of lavender oil (to calm and soothe)

Instructions:

1. Find a quiet space and place your candle at the centre of the heat-proof dish.
2. Arrange the rose quartz, petals and pink salt around it in a small circle.
3. Write your affirmation on the paper, such as: '*I welcome love, joy and connection into my life.*' Fold it three times towards you.
4. Anoint the candle lightly with rose oil and lavender oil.
5. Place the folded paper beneath the candle, light the flame. Pick up the rose quartz and hold it in your hand.
6. Gaze into the flame, breathe deeply and repeat your affirmation three times.
7. Let the candle burn safely for a while, then snuff it out. Carry the rose quartz to keep your heart open and receptive.

EXERCISE: A SIMPLE LOVE RITUAL

If you feel you need to focus on self-love, or would like to attract love in general, use this gentle, simple love ritual. You don't need many tools and this ritual works well after you have completed the ritual to open your heart to love.

You will need:

- A pink candle (for love and self-compassion)
- A rose quartz crystal (or any stone that feels loving to you)
- A few rose petals (fresh or dried)
- A little bit of honey (to sweeten your energy)
- A heat-proof surface or saucer and a lighter or matches

Instructions:

1. Find a quiet place where you won't be disturbed.
2. Light the pink candle and place the rose quartz in front of it.
3. Sprinkle the rose petals around the candle in a circle.
4. Dab a little honey on your heart or lips, saying: '*I welcome love that is kind, true and aligned with my heart.*'
5. Sit quietly for a few minutes, holding the crystal. Imagine yourself surrounded by soft, pink light.
6. When ready, thank the universe (or your guides) and let the candle safely burn out, or snuff it out if needed.

EXERCISE: LOVE & SELF-LOVE REFLECTION

Allow yourself to reflect gently on the nature of love – both the love you give to others in your life and the love you receive.

There is no right or wrong answer.

You may wish to consider:

- What stories, expectations or old beliefs about love am I ready to release?
- Where have I been holding myself back from softness, compassion or care – especially towards myself?
- If love were rooted within me, what might that feel like in my body, my thoughts or my daily life?
- How can I nurture myself with the same patience, kindness and understanding that I so freely offer to others?
- What would it look like to give and receive love with balance, rather than with undue effort or sacrifice?

Let the leaves carry what no longer needs to be held, making space for a more grounded, honest relationship with love – beginning within. Turn the page as you write.

Luck

Luck is often seen as a mysterious and unpredictable force, bringing good fortune into people's lives without clear cause. Across cultures, it has been linked with fate, chance and even divine blessing.

In recent years, scientists have turned their attention to the phenomenon of luck, exploring how mindset and behaviour may influence outcomes. Studies suggest that people who consider themselves lucky often display optimism, openness to new experiences and greater awareness of opportunities.

By cultivating a positive outlook, staying present and acting with confidence, we may increase the chances of favourable events unfolding in our everyday lives.

Magickal correspondences for luck

Colours

- **Green:** prosperity, growth and good fortune in money and opportunity.
- **Gold:** success, abundance and lucky breakthroughs, as well as attracting wealth and blessings.
- **Orange:** new opportunities, confidence and favourable outcomes.

- **Yellow:** joy, clarity and sunny luck; it lifts the spirit to notice opportunities.
- **Red:** courage and vitality. It is often used to draw lucky chances in love and adventure.

Crystals

- **Aventurine:** the stone of opportunity, invites chance encounters and lucky breaks. Choose green aventurine to add strength to abundance and wealth workings.
- **Citrine:** the 'merchant's stone', draws prosperity, abundance and success.
- **Jade:** traditional good-luck charm, offering harmony, wealth and protection.
- **Tiger's eye:** brings courage, confidence and the luck to take bold steps.

Essential oils and incense

- **Cinnamon:** fiery and energising, is used in folk magick to draw wealth, success and quick fortune.
- **Patchouli:** earthy and grounding, is linked with prosperity and attracting opportunities.
- **Jasmine:** uplifting and sensual; used to call in love, joy and lucky encounters.
- **Dragon's blood:** powerful and protective; amplifies intention and magnetises good fortune.
- **Strawberry:** sweet and playful; invites joy, attraction and lucky new beginnings.

- **Frankincense:** sacred and uplifting; traditionally burned to call blessings and divine favour.

Herb, plants and tree allies

- **Basil:** draws prosperity, success and blessings into the home. It was historically kept in the home to invite love and prosperity or given as a token of affection.
- **Bay leaf:** a traditional luck and wish plant; also known as bay laurel.
- **Lemongrass:** clears away stagnant energy and opens the path to new opportunities. Long used in folk charms to draw in luck, success and fresh beginnings or burned in the home to sweep away bad luck and open the way for fortune.
- **Woodruff:** sweetly fragrant and gentle, brings harmony, joy and fortunate encounters. Traditionally scattered on the floor or at festivals to bless places with love and luck. Place a pinch in your left shoe before sports games and your team will be victorious.

Traditionally known as the lucky tree, the rowan (Sorbus aucuparia) was planted near homes and gates to guard against misfortune and invite blessings. Its bright red berries were carried as charms, believed to draw protection, prosperity and good fortune wherever they went.

Spirit animals

- **Frog:** associated with abundance, renewal and lucky transformations.
- **Elephant:** bringer of prosperity, wisdom and enduring good luck.
- **Horse:** a symbol of freedom, progress and lucky breakthroughs on life's path.
- **Butterfly:** transformation, luck in new beginnings and unexpected blessings.

EXERCISE: A SIMPLE BAY LEAF SPELL

This is a simple spell using bay leaves for luck in protection, good fortune, strength and healing.

You will need:

- Pen or marker
- One bay leaf
- A lighter or matches and a heat-proof dish

Instructions:

1. Find a quiet place where you won't be disturbed. Take a moment to settle yourself and ground down into your ritual.
2. Write your wishes or intentions on the bay leaf. Keep it simple and focused, using a few words rather than a long sentence.

3. Place the bay leaf in the heat-proof dish and safely light it to release your intentions through fire. As it burns, focus on the intention you have written, imagining it being released into the flame and carried away with the smoke.
4. Allow the bay leaf to burn fully and cool. When finished, take a quiet breath and return your attention to the present moment. Feel free to bury the remnants in the garden as an offering back to the earth.

You don't even need a spell to tap into the magick of a bay leaf. Here are some simple magickal ways to work with them:

- Place a bay leaf under your pillow for prophetic dreams.
- Place a bay leaf in the corner of a room to protect all who dwell there.
- Carry a bay leaf with you to protect against black magick.
- Place a bay leaf under your mattress to attract your wishes while you sleep.

Write down what it is you would like to wish for below. What might be blocking your luck?

EXERCISE: A SIMPLE LUCK RITUAL

This ritual calls in the energy of fortune, opening the way for opportunities, prosperity and blessings to flow into your life.

You will need:

- 1 green or gold candle (for prosperity and luck) and a lighter or matches
- A pinch of basil or bay leaf (for abundance)
- 1 citrine or aventurine crystal (stones of good fortune)
- Pen and paper
- A few drops of cinnamon or orange oil, diluted

Instructions:

1. Find a quiet space and place your candle in the centre. Arrange the herb and crystal beside it.
2. Write a short affirmation on the paper, such as: '*Luck flows freely into my life. I welcome opportunity and abundance.*'
3. Anoint the candle lightly with the oil and place the folded paper beneath it.
4. Light the candle, focusing on the flame as a beacon drawing good fortune towards you.
5. Hold the crystal in your hand and repeat your affirmation three times. Imagine golden light surrounding you, carrying your intention out into the universe.
6. Let the candle burn safely for a while, then snuff it out. Keep the crystal with you as a charm to carry the energy forwards.

CHAPTER 12

Divination and removal of negative energies

Behold the energies of grounded peace.
We cleanse this space. All harm will cease.
What does not serve or wish us well,
has no more voice, no tale to tell.

In many mystical traditions protection, divination and the removal of negativity are woven together like threads in a sacred tapestry. Before we can receive clear guidance, it is important to create a safe energetic space, shielding ourselves from harmful influences. Divination then becomes a trusted way to glimpse patterns, future choices and hidden truths.

Yet even the clearest vision can be clouded if we carry heavy or stagnant energy, which is why cleansing and banishing practices are equally vital. Together, these arts light our path forwards and ensure we are protected and our spirit remains free from burdensome shadows.

Divination

Since the earliest times, people have sought signs and symbols to help them understand the mysteries of life. Divination is one of the oldest magickal practices. It is a way of listening to the whispers of the universe and interpreting the patterns that lie beneath the surface. At its heart, divination is not about predicting a rigid future or binding us to fate. Instead, it helps us tune into the energies around us so we can navigate with greater wisdom, clarity and confidence.

Magick teaches that the world is alive with meaning. Every shift of energy, every symbol, every ripple in the unseen has something to tell us if we are willing to notice. Divination provides a structure for this noticing. It allows us to pause, step outside of ordinary thinking and engage in dialogue with the deeper currents that shape our lives. This does not mean surrendering responsibility or expecting answers to be handed to us. Rather, it is a partnership between seeker and spirit, a way of aligning our choices with the guidance that already surrounds us.

When we practise divination, we engage both intuition and symbolism. Tools such as tarot cards, runes or pendulums are not inherently magickal in themselves, but they act as mirrors and gateways. Imbued with ancient symbols and archetypal meanings, they give form to the insights already stirring in our subconscious and help us recognise what our inner wisdom has been trying to show us. The cards that fall, the shapes formed in water or flame, the swing of a pendulum: all of these provide a language for the universe to speak.

In magickal practice, divination serves several purposes. It can shine a light on hidden influences that may be affecting a situation and reveal opportunities or challenges that we had not considered. It can also offer reassurance that we are being supported and guided. With this added insight, we may align our intentions more clearly. Once we see the energies at play, we can choose when to act, when to wait and what to release. In this way, divination becomes a tool of empowerment rather than dependency.

Throughout history, many different forms of divination have been practised across cultures. In Celtic tradition, runes and ogham staves carried the wisdom of trees and symbols of the earth. In other traditions, scrying with water, mirrors or crystal balls opened visions of what lay ahead. Tarot, with its rich symbolic imagery, has offered guidance for centuries, while pendulums and dowsing rods have been used to seek clear answers or to locate hidden things. Oracle cards, more modern in form, provide flexible messages of encouragement and reflection.

Each of these methods holds its own rhythm and voice, and part of the journey is discovering which form of divination resonates most strongly with you. As you explore them, remember that the true power lies not in the tool itself but in the connection it awakens between you and the deeper flow of life.

In the following pages, we will explore some of the most accessible and widely used styles of divination. You will gain guidance on how they work and how you can begin to use them in your own practice. Whether you are drawn to the structured symbolism of tarot, the ancient wisdom of runes or the fluid visions of scrying, each path opens a doorway into insight and perspective and deepens your trust in the unseen.

Divination tools

Crystal balls

The crystal ball is a mystical object long associated with divination and inner vision. Rather than offering predictions or absolute answers, it acts as a reflective tool – one that encourages intuition and deep personal insight.

Working with a crystal ball prompts the user to slow down, focus their attention and consider what they would like clarity on. By gazing into the ball, the mind naturally softens. Visions, images, thoughts and emotions can arise. These visions are interpreted and shaped by the individual's intuition, subconscious awareness and, most importantly, lived experience to reflect something personal and unique.

Common questions explored through crystal ball work may relate to many areas of life such as personal growth, relationships, career direction, emotional wellbeing or future possibilities.

It is important to understand that a crystal ball will not reveal fixed outcomes or unavoidable futures. Instead, it brings certain thoughts, feelings and patterns more clearly into focus.

Write your wishes in the crystal ball.

EXERCISE: A MINI CLEANSING RITUAL

Use this ritual before divinatory practices to clear what no longer belongs, so calm and intention may return.

You will need:

- A white candle
- Some incense, preferably lavender
- A rose quartz crystal

Instructions:

1. Light a white candle and let its flame chase away shadows of doubt.
2. Waft lavender or opium incense around you, imagining smoke lifting all heaviness.
3. Hold the rose quartz crystal to your heart, breathing deeply as you release fear.
4. Speak:
   '*I clear the past. I welcome peace. I walk forwards in light.*'
   Remain still for a few moments after speaking.
5. When you feel complete you may allow the candle to burn for a little longer or extinguish it mindfully.

Pendulums

Pendulums are a divination tool for answering questions that have a 'Yes' or 'No' answer. They can assist in weighing your options before an important decision or determining your innermost feelings.

To use a pendulum, prepare a piece of paper or board with 'Yes', 'No' and 'Unclear' marked in three separate places. Hold the chain or cord lightly between your thumb and forefinger, allowing the pendulum to hang freely and remain still. Centre yourself with a few short breaths.

Establish how the pendulum indicates each answer by asking neutral test questions. Once this response is clear, ask focused questions that can be answered simply.

Runes

Rune reading is an ancient form of divination that uses symbols from the Norse alphabet. The runic alphabet was used from the first century onwards to inscribe everything from weapons to household items. As a metaphysical tool, runes were initially used to provide self-knowledge and guidance, helping individuals discover more about themselves, rather than being used as a fortune-telling aid. They were also used on monuments that honoured the dead.

Each rune is associated with a symbolic concept, and thus has its own energy and meaning. There are several language systems associated with runes, but Elder Futhark is the oldest and most common form of runes for divination. Runes for divination are widely available in many metaphysical shops, but you may wish to inscribe your own runes by writing the alphabet on specially collected pebbles.

EXERCISE: A THREE-RUNE READING

You will need:

- A clear area to throw runes
- A bag of Elder Futhark runes

Instructions:

1. To begin, find a quiet space where you can focus without distraction.
2. Ground yourself with a few deep breaths. Hold your rune bag in both hands, asking clearly for guidance on your question.
3. Draw three runes from the bag and place them in a row, left to right. The first represents the past or the foundation of your situation. The second shows the present influences. The third offers future guidance or outcome.
4. Take time to study each rune's symbol and traditional meaning. Notice also your intuition: what feelings or images arise as you hold them? Runes often work as much through personal insight as through memorised definitions.
5. Once you have reflected on the spread, thank the runes for their guidance and return them to the bag.

It's important to know that rune readings rarely give absolute answers. Instead, they shine a light on the currents around you, helping you see options more clearly and strengthening trust in your own inner wisdom.

Write the result of your rune reading here.

How does this resonate with you?

Tarot cards

Tarot is all about trusting our own intuition. Reading cards pushes us to listen to our inner voice and have confidence in the guidance it provides. By doing so, we can make decisions that are aligned with our true selves and lead us to greater fulfilment.

EXERCISE: A BASIC TAROT SPREAD

A three-card spread is one of the most accessible and versatile ways to read tarot cards. To begin, shuffle the deck while focusing on your question. Draw three cards and place them in a row from left to right.

- **Card 1, past:** represents the influences or experiences leading to this moment.
- **Card 2, present:** reflects the energy, challenges, or opportunities surrounding you now.
- **Card 3, future:** reveals likely outcomes or guidance on the path ahead.

This simple yet powerful spread offers clarity and insight, and a clear narrative to guide your next steps. Find more suggested spreads on the following pages.

Tarot vs oracle cards

Tarot can sometimes feel like reading a book with set chapters and archetypes, while oracle cards are more like poetry: fluid, adaptable and unique to the specific deck, yet still offering guidance, clarity and inspiration. Many diviners use both together, letting tarot give structure and oracle cards add supportive, expansive insights.

Oracle sets are usually built on a similar principle to tarot cards, but unlike tarot, which follows a structured system of 78 cards divided into the Major and Minor Arcana, oracle decks can take almost any form. Each deck has its own theme – angels, animals, goddesses, affirmations or any theme chosen by the creator.

Oracle cards act like a conversation with spirit, offering encouragement, direction or gentle reminders of the energies surrounding you. Their messages usually contain keywords, phrases or imagery designed to spark intuition, which makes them excellent for quick guidance, daily pulls or when you want gentle encouragement and clarity. The messages are also often easier to interpret, making them ideal for beginners.

To use the oracle cards, simply shuffle the deck while focusing on a question or intention, then draw one or more cards.

Other tarot and oracle spreads

Mind – Body – Spirit

Card 1, mind: What the mind is holding onto.
Card 2, body: The state of the body or physical world.
Card 3, spirit: The spirit's guidance.

Situation – Challenge – Advice

Card 1, situation: The core of the issue.
Card 2, challenge: What stands in the way.
Card 3, advice: Guidance for moving forward.

Choice A – Choice B – Guidance

Card 1, choice A: Path one and where it may lead.
Card 2, choice B: Path two and its possibilities.
Card 3, guidance: Higher guidance to support your decision.

Releasing a tricky situation

Card 1: The root of the situation.
Card 2: The current state of affairs.
Card 3: The future of the situation.

Scrying

Scrying is a form of divination that involves gazing into a reflective surface to receive insight or symbolic imagery. Traditionally this may include gazing upon water in a bowl, a mirror or darkened glass, or looking deeply into a crystal, a polished stone or the flame of a candle.

Rather than seeing literal images, scrying often works through intuition, imagination and subtle perception. The mind softens its focus allowing symbols, feelings or thoughts to surface. Scrying is less about predicting the future and more about listening inward, using stillness and reflection as a way to access deeper awareness.

Magickal correspondences for divination

Colours

- **Purple:** opens psychic awareness, intuition and connection to higher wisdom.
- **Indigo/dark blue:** encourages deep focus, calm insight and spiritual vision.
- **White:** universal clarity, truth and purity of guidance.
- **Black:** grounds energy, banishes confusion and protects against unwanted influence.

Crystals

- **Amethyst:** opens the third eye, calms the mind and deepens intuitive vision.
- **Labradorite:** enhances psychic awareness and dream recall, and offers protection during spiritual work.
- **Moonstone:** connects to lunar energy, intuition and feminine wisdom; aids dream journeys.
- **Clear quartz:** amplifies intention, clarity and spiritual communication.

Essential oils and incense

- **Peppermint:** sharpens focus, clears the mind and awakens inner sight.
- **Lemon:** brightens energy, lifts mental fog and brings clarity to readings.

- **Jasmine:** enhances intuition, dreamwork and spiritual connection.
- **Dragon's blood:** strengthens protection, raises energy and empowers divinatory rituals.

Herb, plant and tree allies

- **Lovage:** once added to baths and brews to heighten attraction and perception; thought to stir prophetic dreams of love.
- **Mugwort:** the classic seer's herb, burned or placed under the pillow to invite visions and enhance psychic sight.
- **Thyme:** place under the pillow to encourage dreams of prophecy and guidance.
- **Willow:** associated with the moon and water, deepening intuition and helping seers move between worlds.
- **Hazel:** tree of wisdom and insight. Hazelnuts were believed to contain all knowledge, guiding seers to truth.
- **Creeping cinquefoil:** slipped under the pillow to dream of future love or answers, opening visions through sleep.

Spirit animals

Spirit animals are important allies in divination as companions, guides, protectors and messengers from the unseen realms. They may appear within dreams and meditations, or even in everyday life, so pay attention to what animals cross your path. Witches call on spirit animals during readings (e.g. invoking the owl for wisdom or the wolf for guidance) and honour them with imagery, feathers, carvings or symbolic representations in their ritual space.

Meditate on which protective animal calls you. Place items that resonate with that animal on your altar. Call upon them during rituals for shielding and guidance.

- **Owl:** wisdom and seeing beyond. Owls are known as seers of the night and represent intuition, prophecy and the ability to see through illusion.
- **Wolf:** guidance and instinct. The wolf, a symbol of intuition, particularly supports divination that involves guidance for life's journey.
- **Deer/stag:** wisdom, sovereignty and initiation. In Celtic lore, the deer or stag guides seekers between worlds.
- **Eagle/hawk:** vision and prophecy. They are excellent for divination when clarity and truth are needed, or when we need to see the bigger picture.

EXERCISE: WAX SCRYING RITUAL

To receive gentle insights, allow your subconscious and intuition to surface softly. Wax scrying reveals what is forming, not what is fixed, and so is best used for reflection, guidance and pattern recognition rather than fixed outcomes.

You will need:

- A small candle (any colour) and a lighter or matches
- A bowl of cold water
- A journal and a pen

Instructions:

1. Take three slow breaths to calm your mind.
2. Set a simple intention, such as '*Show me what is forming.*'
3. Light the candle and hold it so the wax drips into the water.
4. The wax will harden in the water. When it sets, remove it from the water and observe its shape from different angles.
5. What do you see? Notice feelings, images and impressions rather than forcing a meaning. In your journal, note what the image may reflect in your current life, its shape and form. How does it resonate with you right now?
6. Extinguish the candle to close the practice.

Protection magick

Protection magick not only shields your body and home, it weaves light around the spirit as a sacred guard against the unseen tides that can press upon us. It is to draw a circle of intention that says: '*Here, only harmony may enter. Here, only truth may stay.*'

Protection keeps our energy intact, our thoughts clear and our hearts steady as we walk the pathways of spellwork and ritual. Without protection, the open gates of magick may invite not only inspiration, but also confusion, unwanted influences or the draining pull of others. To guard ourselves is not fear: it is wisdom. It is honouring the boundaries that let us work with power safely and enduring strength.

I remember one evening when protection became more than theory to me. I had been working with herbs and candles, learning to open myself to the currents of energy. That openness, though beautiful, left me restless at night, as if the air itself hummed with too many voices. I crafted a simple charm: a small pouch of rosemary, black tourmaline and salt, tied with a ribbon. I placed it beneath my pillow and that night, the heaviness lifted.

My dreams grew peaceful, the whispers grew silent, and I woke with a calm heart. Since then, I never begin spellwork without first creating a shield – be it smoke from sage, a whispered incantation or a circle of candles. Protection is the anchor of all magick, the quiet promise that we are safe as we reach into mystery. It allows us to explore the unseen, knowing that we return to ourselves whole.

What do you need protection from? Write them in the clouds.

Magickal correspondences for protection

Protection is not only about shielding from harm, but also strengthening your own energy so that you walk with clarity, calm and confidence

Colours

- **White:** universal light of purity and protection. Use a white candle to establish a sacred circle, burn away negativity and invite peace.
- **Black:** powerful protection, banishes negativity and absorbs unwanted energy. Burn a black candle to create a shield of safety, grounding the spirit and dispelling harmful influence.

Crystals

- **Clear quartz:** amplifies all protective work, redirecting harmful energy and enhancing the power of herbs, oils and incantations in its proximity.
- **Black tourmaline:** a powerful stone of protection. It shields against negativity and harmful energies. It was traditionally kept at doorways or carried on the body to ground the spirit and ward off ill will.

Essential oils and incense

- **Cinnamon:** fiery defender that banishes negativity and strengthens personal courage.

- **Dragon's blood:** intensifies protective spells, sealing intentions with fiery energy.
- **Lemon:** purifies spaces, sharpens the mind and guards against intrusive energies.

Herb, plant and tree allies

- **Rowan:** known as the witch's tree, planted by doorways to guard against ill fortune
- **Hawthorn:** sacred to the fae, its branches were kept to protect the home and heart
- **Angelica root:** carried as a charm to protect from sickness and dark influences.
- **Nettle:** hung at the door to keep away danger and unwelcome spirits.
- **Garlic:** a household protector, said to repel evil and misfortune.

Spirit animals

Many spirit animals are associated with protective energies that shield us from harm and walk beside us when strength is needed. These spirit allies remind us that we are never alone in facing darkness.

- **Owl:** sees through deception and illusion, shields the witch during divination and spiritual work, and protects them in the darkness, guiding with wisdom.

- **Wolf:** fierce protector and loyal guardian, defends against energetic intrusion and brings courage and clarity of instinct.
- **Hawk/eagle:** watchful guardians with sharp vision who protect from unseen dangers and harmful influences. They encourage clear perspective in times of confusion.
- **Stag/deer:** guardian of thresholds and otherworldly journeys, protects sacred space and personal sovereignty, and guides the soul safely between realms.

EXERCISE: DIVINE YOUR SPIRIT ANIMAL

Meditate on which protective animal calls to you. Place images, feathers or symbols of that animal on your altar. Call upon them during rituals for shielding and guidance.

EXERCISE: CREATE A PROTECTION SACHET

You will need:

- A bay leaf
- Some fresh or dried mint
- Some basil
- A pinch of cinnamon powder or a cinnamon stick
- A small bag or scrap of cloth with twine. For an extra boost of protection use a black pouch
- A protective crystal if you have one, such as black onyx, snowflake obsidian or clear quartz

Instructions:

1. Begin by grounding yourself and setting a clear intention for protection.
2. Place the herbs into the sachet, acknowledging their protective qualities.
3. Add the crystal, visualising it strengthening and anchoring your protection.
4. Tie the sachet, imagining its contents working together as a shield.
5. Carry the sachet with you or place it wherever protection is needed.

EXERCISE: PROTECTION SPELL JAR

You will need:

- A small glass jar
- Incense (rosemary, sage or dragon's blood would work well)
- A piece of black onyx
- Black salt
- Rosemary essential oil, if available
- Pen and paper

Instructions:

1. **Prepare your jar.** Cleanse a small glass jar by wafting incense smoke around and inside of the jar. Hold the jar in your hands and set the intention of protection.
2. **Add the protection stone.** Place a piece of black onyx inside the jar. This stone is traditionally seen as a strong shield against negativity and unwanted influences.

3. **Seal with salt and scent.** Cover the stone with a layer of black salt for protection, then add a few drops of rosemary essential oil for purification.
4. **Set the intention.** On a slip of paper, write an affirmation such as:
   '*I am safe, protected and surrounded by light.*' Place it inside the jar.
5. **Seal the practice.** Close the lid, and keep it near your doorway, altar or carry it with you for continual protection.

EXERCISE: SAFE DRIVING PROTECTION AMULET

You will need:

- Black salt
- Black pepper
- A small bag
- A protection crystal, such as black onyx or obsidian
- Pen and paper

Instructions:

1. Prepare black salt by either mixing salt with incense ash and charcoal or mixing salt with a few drops of black food dye.
2. Combine the black pepper and the black salt in the small bag.
3. Place your protection crystal into the bag, making sure it is entirely covered.
4. For extra power, write an intention on a piece of paper, fold it and bury it in the bag. Examples of intentions can be:

'I travel safely and arrive protected.'
'My path is clear and my driving is calm.'
'I am protected in this vehicle and on this road.'
'I return home safely each time I travel.'

5. Hang the bag in your car.

EXERCISE: CIRCLE OF PROTECTION

The circle of protection is an imagined boundary of pure white light, created to hold and safeguard whatever you place within it.

Visualise a circle forming around you, glowing brightly. Know that nothing harmful can cross its edge.

Within this space, you, your tools or your intentions are shielded from negativity and outside interference. The circle is not just a barrier but also a sacred container, amplifying the energy you raise and focusing it clearly.

Whether used for meditation, ritual or everyday peace of mind, the circle offers safety, balance and a sense of spiritual empowerment.

Draw a magickal circle. Write in the names of those you wish to protect within it.

Banishing negative energies

Everything in this world carries energy, and just as dust gathers in the corners of a home, heavy or stagnant vibrations can collect in our minds, bodies and living spaces.

Negative energies do not always announce themselves dramatically. Often they arrive quietly: a sharp word that lingers in the air, a place that feels off for no reason, the drain of being around those who take more than they give. Over time, these subtle imprints weigh us down, clouding clarity, dampening joy and leaving us restless.

To banish these energies is not superstition, but self-care. Just as we cleanse our skin with water, so too must we refresh our spirit with light. Clearing negativity is an act of renewal and a way of opening the windows of the soul to let in fresh air. It returns us to balance and makes room for peace, creativity and healing to flourish. In magickal practice, this is considered a form of banishing – clearing away unwanted or stagnant energies.

I remember a time when my shop felt unusually heavy. The air was thick and sales were stagnant. Even my own mood seemed caught in a low current. I trusted my instinct that the energy needed lifting. I lit a white candle, burned a blend of rosemary and sandalwood, and carried the smoke through every corner. With each step, I whispered an intention: '*Only light remains, only love endures.*'

By the time I finished, the air felt lighter, as if a weight had been lifted. Regular customers who had not visited in weeks appeared later that day and I felt joy return to the space. It reminded me that energy is as real as the air we breathe and that tending to it is a simple yet powerful form of magick.

Clearing negativity is how we honour ourselves, how we make room for light to enter once more.

Magickal correspondences for banishing negative energies

Colours

- **White:** purity, clarity and divine protection.
- **Black:** removes and absorbs negative energy. Burn black candles to banish negativity and shield energy.
- **Green:** healing, renewal and prosperity.
- **Red:** vitality, courage and strength.

Crystals

- **Amethyst:** spiritual protection, intuition and calm.
- **Black tourmaline:** grounding and warding off negativity.
- **Rose quartz:** love, compassion and emotional healing.
- **Citrine:** abundance, joy and vitality.

Essential oils and incense

- **Dragon's blood:** powerful protection and energy amplifier.
- **Rosemary:** clarity, cleansing and strength.
- **Ylang-ylang:** balance, emotional harmony and attraction.
- **Frankincense:** sacred, uplifting and spiritually protective.

Herb, plant and tree allies

- **Angelica root:** a guardian herb, traditionally carried in charms or burned to drive out harmful forces.
- **Bay leaf:** removes negativity. Write what you wish to release on a leaf and cast into flame.
- **Eucalyptus leaves:** sweeps away stagnant energy and clears the air after conflict.
- **Horehound:** protects against harmful magick, breaks hexes and supports strength.
- **Woodruff:** protective and luck-bringing; used in charms to keep away negativity.
- **Oak bark:** symbol of strength and endurance; wards off dark or draining energies.
- **Rowan:** a traditional protective tree, associated with banishing ill luck or enchantment.

Rosemary (Salvia rosmarinus) is one of the oldest cleansing herbs, long used to banish negativity and protect sacred space. Its sharp invigorating scent clears stagnant energy, purifies the mind and strengthens spiritual boundaries, making it a trusted ally in rituals of protection and renewal. Sprigs were placed under pillows to ward off nightmares and protect sleep.

How to use banishing herbs

Throughout folklore and magickal practice, plants and trees have been allies in cleansing spaces and warding off harmful influence. Their living spirit holds power to banish heaviness and restore harmony.

- Hang sprigs of rosemary, bay leaf or eucalyptus in your home for ongoing cleansing.
- Burn dried lemongrass, horehound or rosemary in an incense blend.
- Carry a small pouch of rowan berries, oak bark and angelica root as a protective charm.
- Use willow or alder wood to craft wands or staffs for protection during rituals.

EXERCISE: CREATE YOUR OWN BANISHING OIL

Banishing oil is a powerful magickal tool charged to drive away negativity, unhealthy attachments and unwanted influences. Just as smoke clears a room or water washes the body, banishing oil clears the subtle layers of the spirit.

Remember, banishing is not about fear or superstition, but about reclaiming your space and energy. Banishing is both shield and sword, a reminder that your space is sacred and that you hold the power to keep it clear.

You will need:

- A pinch each of protective herbs such as rosemary, bay leaf and black pepper
- A small piece of angelica root
- A drop of dragon's blood resin, if available
- A small, dark glass bottle
- 2 tablespoons of skin-safe base oil (such as olive, jojoba or almond)
- Essential oils: 2 drops each of clove, cinnamon, eucalyptus, and lemon

Instructions:

1. Begin by grounding yourself and setting your intention clearly:
   '*With this oil I banish all that harms and all drains, all that does not belong.*'
2. Place the herbs and roots into your bottle. Pour the base oil all over them slowly, imagining a circle of protective light forming around you. Add the essential oils drop by drop, whispering your intention as you do so.
3. Seal the bottle tightly and shake gently to blend. Keep in a cool, dark place. The oil will grow stronger as it infuses over several days.

Uses:

- Anoint candles and tools for banishing rituals.
- Dab on thresholds such as door frames and windows to protect your home.
- Wear a tiny amount (diluted) on the wrists and soles of the feet to maintain personal boundaries.

EXERCISE: CORD CUTTING RITUAL

The purpose of cord cutting is to disconnect your energy from another person.

You will need:

- A toothpick, safety pin or needle for inscribing on the candle
- 2 candles in colours that correspond to your intention
- Banishing oil or ritual oil, if available
- A pinch of banishing herbs, if available
- String or twine of a natural material
- A lighter or matches and a heat-proof dish

Instructions:

1. Using the toothpick, carve your name into one of the candles and the other person's name on the other.

2. If you have banishing oil and herbs, dress the candles. Rub the oil in an upward motion and roll the candles in the banishing herbs.
3. Tie one end of the string around the middle of one candle. Tie the other end of the string around the second candle. There should be a small distance between the candles, but the string should be tight between them.
4. Place the candles in a heat-proof dish.
5. Take a deep breath and mentally prepare yourself for this disconnection.
6. Light the candles.
7. As you watch the string burn, visualise your connection being released. The tie between is breaking.
8. Sit with the candles until they burn down, softly interpreting the way they burn and the messages of the flame. Journal about this for reference for later.
9. Bury the remaining candle stubs in the earth.

QUICK MINI RITUALS TO CUT NEGATIVE TIES

Take a slip of paper and pen, write what it is you wish to let go of, then release the energy in one of these ways:

- Bury the paper in the earth.
- Cut the paper into pieces.
- Burn it in a candle flame.
- Cleanse with palo santo or sage.
- Circle the paper with salt and leave it for 24 hours before burning.

EXERCISE: A SIMPLE BANISHING RITUAL

1. **Name what no longer serves you.** Write several sentences beginning with '*I am ready to release*'. Let your mind flow freely. Do not justify or explain, simply let the list be blunt and honest. This identifies what needs to be banished.
2. **The cost of carrying it.** Divide a page in your journal into two columns. Left column: '*What this has taken from me.*' Right column: '*What becomes possible when I let it go.*' This clarifies motivation and prevents banishing from becoming avoidance.
3. **Write it out of your system.** Write a letter addressed to the following:

    - a habit
    - a fear
    - a belief
    - a situation
    - an old version of yourself.

4. **Banish it with speech.** Say everything you would never say out loud, do not re-read it. At the end, write: '*This no longer has power over me.*' You may later burn or tear up the page if that feels appropriate.

What would your life story be called?

____

____

Fill the clouds with positive thoughts. Some have been suggested for you already.

I am worthy of abundance, joy and success.

A daily ritual is a way of saying, 'I am putting myself first. I have to look after myself, so that I can look after others.'

Bravery is the audacity to be unhindered by failures.

Afterword

Just as weeds can overrun the soil and prevent blossoms from reaching the light, old hurts and lingering shadows can choke the heart. By tending gently to your inner garden – watering it with kindness, pruning away what no longer serves – you create fertile ground for new joys, friendships and opportunities to flourish. Letting go of old tales is not about forgetting them, but about releasing their grip so that new and wondrous stories may take root.

Forge ahead with a clarity of mind and a purposeful heart. Survival asks us only to get through the day. Thriving invites us to live fully, boldly and with intention. When we choose to rise beyond old fears and doubts, our path straightens before us, clear and strong. With each step, we move closer to our true self, carrying only what nourishes and uplifts us.

If you have read this far, then you already know that magick is not something that exists outside of you. It is within you, threaded through your every breath, your thoughts, your small rituals of daily life. To practise practical magick is not to step into a fantasy: it is to step into yourself.

Over the years, as I've shared this work with customers, friends and fellow seekers, I've lost count of how many times someone has lowered their voice and said: *'You'll think I'm mad'* or *'This must be a stupid question'*. I often smile gently, because most of the time, I already know exactly what they're going to say before the words even leave their mouth. I know because I have been there myself. I've stood in the same place, wondering if I was odd for feeling the presence of a tree, or for believing that herbs and crystals could heal more than just the body.

But here is the truth I want to leave you with: this is not madness. This is a way of life. Practical magick is about living in rhythm with the world around us. It's about honouring the cycle of nature: the turning of seasons, the phases of the moon, the ebb and flow of light and dark. It's about choosing to see meaning where others see only accident, to weave intention where others move without thought. What harm is there in that? None.

Our guiding principle has always been the same: *harm no one.*

That is the root, the branch and the leaf of this path.

You do not need permission to live this way. You do not need approval from a teacher, a community or even from me, the author of this book. You only need to listen to your heart, to your intuition, to the subtle nudges of the universe that whisper: this is for you.

You are already enough.

Your magick is yours to claim.

When I look back on my own journey, I see how magick walked with me even before I had words for it. As a child, I would gather leaves, flowers and herbs from the garden and make potions, stirring them together with a deep sense of wonder.

I didn't know then that I was already weaving the first threads of a lifelong connection. Later, when life became heavy and responsibilities weighed down, I returned to those simple acts – lighting a candle, whispering an intention, blending oils and herbs – and discovered that these small rituals held enormous power.

They lifted me, guided me and reminded me of who I was.

Closing notes

As you close these pages, remember that magick is already woven through your daily life. Every candle lit with intention, every herb scattered on the floor, every crystal carried in your pocket is an act of quiet power.

Throughout this book, you have met trees that whisper wisdom, herbs that soothe the heart, crystals that heal and candles that illuminate the way. Their presence is more than symbolic. They carry with them centuries of lore and the voices of those who came before us. Folk traditions like the following remind us that magick has always belonged to the people:

- Sit beneath the willow to let sorrow flow away.
- Carry an acorn for strength and steady love.
- Scatter meadowsweet to sweeten the home and quiet quarrels.
- Burn rosemary to chase away ill winds and call in renewal.
- Place a bay leaf beneath your pillow to dream of your heart's desire.

These traditions are simple, yet they hold deep truth. They remind us that we do not need grand rituals to walk in magick, only the willingness to notice, to honour and to act with intention.

Whenever you feel uncertain, cast a circle of white light, placing within it all you wish to protect. When you feel heavy, light a black candle and let its flame absorb what no longer serves you. When you feel open to guidance, draw a card or rune, or simply step beneath a tree and listen. The universe speaks in many voices: divination, protection and cleansing are all ways of clearing the path so you can hear it more clearly.

So take what you have found here and weave it into your own path. As you light your candles, blend your herbs and write your affirmations, trust the quiet knowing that arises within you. You are not alone on this journey. You walk it alongside the wisdom of the earth, the strength of your ancestors and the guiding hand of spirit.

May your steps be grounded, your heart at peace, your path protected and your life filled with magick.

Further reading

If you'd like to continue exploring beyond these pages, here are some wonderful books that offer deeper insights and practical guidance on magick, herbs, crystals, and spiritual practice.

Cunningham, Scott. *The Complete Book of Incense, Oils & Brews*. Llewellyn Worldwide, 2002.

A classic guide to creating your own incense blends, oils, brews and magickal preparations using natural ingredients.

Harner, Michael J. *The Way of the Shaman*. 10th edition. HarperCollins, 1997.

A groundbreaking work that introduces the principles and practices of shamanism, guiding readers into deeper spiritual connection.

Judith, Anodea. *Wheels of Life: A User's Guide to the Chakra System*. 2nd edition. Llewellyn Worldwide, 1999.

A definitive book on the chakras, blending psychology, spirituality and practical exercises for balance and healing

Neal, Carl F. *Incense: Crafting & Use of Magickal Scents*. 2nd edition. Llewellyn Worldwide, 2026.

An in-depth look at the history, creation and magickal uses of incense blends, resins and rituals.

Webster, Richard. *How to Use a Crystal*. Llewellyn Worldwide, 2019.

A simple yet powerful introduction to crystals, their properties and how to work with them for healing and spiritual growth.

Webster, Richard. *The Secret to Attracting Luck*. Llewellyn Worldwide, 2021.

A practical and inspiring book on drawing good fortune, opportunity and synchronicity into your life.

Worwood, Valerie Ann. *The Fragrant Mind: Aromatherapy for Personality, Mind, Mood and Emotion*. Random House, 1997.

An exploration of aromatherapy and essential oils, focusing on their influence on emotions, intuition and spiritual wellbeing.

Name the books you wish to read in the book spines below.

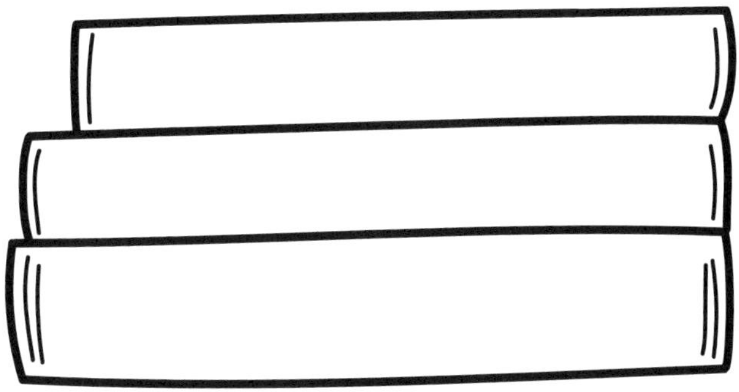

What do you want to learn more about? Note your final reflections below.

About the author

Hazel Cahill is a qualified yoga teacher, sound therapist, and shamanic practitioner. She integrates Druidic and Celtic traditions, shamanism and earth-based spiritual practices into her therapies and her magickal store in Kildare, Ireland. Hazel offers a variety of crystals, magickal herbs, incense and accessories to curious customers whom she encounters daily.

pureandsimple.ie
pureandsimple_magicalstore
pureandsimpleholistics